SIR EDWARD ELGAR

JOHN FIELDER PORTE

WITH A PORTRAIT OF SIR EDWARD ELGAR
AND
MUSICAL ILLUSTRATIONS IN THE TEXT,

 BOOKS FOR LIBRARIES PRESS
FREEPORT, NEW YORK

First Published 1921
Reprinted 1970

STANDARD BOOK NUMBER:
8369-5194-8

LIBRARY OF CONGRESS CATALOG CARD NUMBER
75-107827

PRINTED IN THE UNITED STATES OF AMERICA

THE Author desires to tender his thanks for information
courteously given by :—Dr A. Eaglefield Hull, Dr Frederick
J. Karn, Mr Landon Ronald, Mr Harvey Grace (" Musical
Times "), Mr Robin H. Legge, Mr W. Elkin (Messrs Elkin
and Co.), Miss Margaret Fairless, Messrs Boosey and Co.,
Ltd., Messrs Enoch and Co., Ltd., The Gramophone Co.,
Ltd., Messrs Novello and Co., Ltd., Messrs Joseph Williams
and Co., " The Bath and Wilts Chronicle."

CONTENTS

ELGARIAN MAXIMS

" *When I see one of my works by the side of, say, the Fifth Symphony, I feel as a tinker might do when he sees the Forth Bridge.*" (Note.—This remark was made before Elgar's own symphonies had appeared, although his attitude towards Beethoven always remained the same.)

. . . . "*the creative artist suffers in creating, or in contemplating the unending influence of his creation. Yes, suffers; this is the only word I dare use, for even the highest ecstacy of ' Making,' is mixed with the consciousness of the sombre dignity of the eternity of the artist's responsibility.*"

" *I do not think that among those persons who are able to pay liberally for music, a love of music has grown very much, but among those who are not able to pay for luxuries the love of good choral music and good orchestral music has grown by leaps and bounds.*"

. . . " *the highest kind of music, with its soothing, elevating and beneficient influences.*"

" *English orchestral players are second to none.*"

" *I would like you to think seriously whether the humanising sphere of music could not be enlarged by municipal aid—by assisting choral societies and orchestras from the rates.*"

" *We ought to bring the best music to the people who are least able to pay for it.*"

" *The time is coming when all towns must be able to give the people the good music they want.*"

" *Under existing circumstances it too often is a matter of ery special enterprise to get up a well-equipped performance of a large work. This should not be ; larger halls are necessary, and sooner or later municipal aid is bound to be given."* (Note.—This, and the preceding remarks on the assisting of musical bodies by local councils, were made before the Labour Party had widely advertised the support of music from the rates as being part of their programme.)

" The new education should include music in the widest sense and tend to create listeners—not merely executants ; this can best be accomplished by means of the Gramophone."

" Early experience is required to endow audiences with understanding and appreciation ; therefore it is desirable that old-fashioned and worse than useless trifling with the keyboard should give place to reasonable and easily attainable methods." (Note.—This is a further reference to the Gramophone.)

" I regard a concert hall as essential to every town."

" I am intensely very grateful for any interest taken in my work."

" The symphony without a programme is the highest development of the art."

" The Third Symphony of Brahms is the height of music." (Note.—This statement was made with reference to the *absolute* quality of the work.)

" Music which exists without any poetic or literary basis is the foundation of the art."

" Cultivate the love of music for its own sake."

" Programme music is essentially the literary man's attitude towards an art with which he has sympathy, but of which his knowledge is comparatively small."

" The worship of technique is regretable, the musician needs education and experience. There is no authority in uncultured players, however skilful, neither is there in very youthful artists, however clever."

" I would go a hundred miles to hear a Wagner Opera."

SIR EDWARD ELGAR

CRITICAL INTRODUCTION

On his own showing, Elgar was a purist, but the assertion that he wrote in the language of the past is very near a fallacy. With him music was music only and a medium of expression rather than description. He had no use for programme or electrifying effects because they naturally stood in the way of his altruistic principles. We have ample proof that he did not hug the classical traditions for their own sake, in the oratorio *Gerontius*. Here the established form, and it was at the time of the production of the work, as it still is now, very firmly established, stood in the way of his desire for expressive and living characters. It is now common knowledge how he cast away traditions in a manner that shocked and be-wildered the English public, but was recognised by Strauss and others in Germany as a master stroke.

The whole aspect of the greater creative Elgar is condensed into the fact that he was Elgar and nobody else. It is not a question of which school he was or was not a member, for his foremost desire was to

make music that was a living force—a something
that would be understood and exist solely by its
power of expression. He made exceptions, but his
greatest works, as he has told us, were conceived with
his ideal always in view. Elgar has none of the
classic and purist stagnancy that unfortunately often
appears in Brahms, for he was inoculated against it
with a remarkable power and originality of personal
appeal.

In our wise moments we speak of Bach as a contrapuntalist, Beethoven as a classic and Wagner as a
romantic, but what really matters is that they all
wrote music that has the power to grip our emotional
senses. We may call Wagner a Church-music writer
and Beethoven a Futurist, but it does not alter the
fundamental power of their creations. It is admitted
that the art of expression in music-making has developed enormously since the days of Bach, but the
spirit of humanity is felt as clearly amid the technical
maze of this composer as it is in the exquisite poetry
of Chopin. It is not Bach the contrapuntalist, or
Beethoven the classic, that the music-lover listens to,
but Bach and Beethoven the men. The schools of
these composers belong essentially to the past; but
music of the heart will outlive music of the brain
alone. The history book will show us that Beethoven
was in his lifetime one of the many classics ; now,
with perhaps Mozart, he stands as the only classic.

It has been said that Elgar infused new life into

the tottering form, but this will not make him immortal any more than if he had been an extreme
modernist, for either factor would eventually become
of nothing more than academical interest if they
stood alone.

In no sense do we wish to decry the technical side
of music, for without a mastery of it the most talented
musician will quickly find his development restricted.
On the other hand, however, it is impossible to bolster
up for long any music or musicians having only
technical significance. There are many of the large
symphonic works by modern composers which are
constructed with nothing short of a consummate
mastery of technique. In performance they even
sound very fine, but there always appears to be
something missing. They lack the " divine fire "
that stirs our innermost feelings and lifts us to a more
sublime realisation of what music really is.

It is really impossible to say whether Elgar will
command the admiration of the future as he does that
of to-day, but those who know the *Adagio* and the
glorious final pages of his first symphony, and the
slow movements of the pianoforte quintet and second
symphony, will know why we entertain the highest
hopes of Elgar becoming, as far as his greater works
are concerned, one of the immortals, entirely irre-
spective of nationality.

HIS CAREER

EDWARD WILLIAM ELGAR was born on June 2nd, 1857, at Broadheath, about four miles from Worcester, England. His parents appear to have come from thoroughly English stock, the father being a native of Dover and the mother a member of a yeoman family of Herefordshire. W. H. Elgar, the father, was a musician both in trade and spirit, having a music shop in Worcester and in his remaining time being a violinist in a local orchestra, and organist at the Roman Catholic Church of St. George. He cherished a great love for the great classic masters, especially Mozart and Beethoven. He was also instrumental in bringing about the performances of Masses by Cherubini and Hummel at the famous Three Choirs' Festival, Worcester.

The birthplace of Edward is in the neighbourhood of the Malvern Hills, and it is easy to find the spirit of these bold elevations, with their invigorating air, historical traditions and beautiful views, in the composer's earlier big works. Although the father recognised his son's talent as the latter grew along, he was unable to afford him any special guidance, so the boy was left mostly to his own devices as far as music was concerned. Apart from a number of lessons on the violin and tinkerings on the pianoforte, Edward received no real musical instruction, and laborious drudging and indomitable self-tuition made the foundation stones of the long looked for emancipator of British music. This grinding struggle for knowledge was the early indication of Elgar's tremendous power of self-assertion. It was the infantile beginning of his tenacious and all-conquering march towards his great ideal, the making of music as a pure and sincere medium of self-expression ; the cultivation of the love of music for its own sake, without the aid of poetical subject matter.

A distinct benefit that young Edward received was the availability for him of various musical instruments, and this may well have been the foundation of his love and inimitable understanding of the orchestra. He played the bassoon in a wind quintet, for which he is accredited to have written music, but he was most successful with the violin, which led him to positions in orchestras and appearances as a soloist. In addition to his musical self-study, he was a great reader of good literature, and in a stable loft he treasured some, to him, priceless works. This taste he doubtless inherited from his mother, who was a scholarly woman, with a taste for the higher things of this life. One other point in Elgar's early life must not be overlooked, and that is his opportunities for listening to, and playing on, his father's organ at church, but he had to travel 250 miles to hear a London Orchestral Concert, starting at 6 a.m., and returning at 10.30 p.m.

The composer's school life does not seem to have been very eventful, for being a born student he cared little for games. On entering the school, which was called Littleton House, the headmaster asked him his name, and young Edward replied, " Edward Elgar." " Add the word ' Sir ! ' " said the school-master, sharply. The reply came meekly, but prophetically, " Sir Edward Elgar." Needless to say the dominie did not appreciate the prophecy to this extent. However, he did the future composer a good turn later on by telling his pupils the story of the Apostles, and it was the schoolmaster's remarks that were directly responsible for the germ of the great oratorio *The Apostles*, which appeared over thirty years later. When Edward left school he went into a solicitor's office, but we can well imagine how he felt there, and after a year he came back to help the musical activities of his father.

One of the most important factors in the moulding of Elgar's youth was his association with the Worcester Glee Club, in the activities of which he appeared as violinist, pianoforte accompanist, conductor and composer. In 1878 he was presented with a violin bow in recognition of his services, in spite of the fact that some of the " old men " alleged that he put some rather weird harmonies into his accompaniments at times. During all this interpretative work, he worked unceasingly at " making " music, and although he was not deemed a prodigy, the production, when he was past fifty years of age, of the *Wand of Youth* music, proved to the astonished world of admirers that he was something of this nature at the tender age of twelve.

After much thought, Elgar abandoned his idea of becoming a solo-violinist, visited Leipzig and in 1885 succeeded his father as organist of St. George's Church, Worcester. This latter appointment he resigned in 1889, and in the same year married Caroline Alice, daughter of Major-General Sir Henry Gee Roberts, K.C.B. Elgar's wife admired and believed in his genius, and became something more than a looker on by writing poetry for his songs, giving up literary successes in other forms and helping him considerably with his orchestral scoring.

After his marriage, Elgar removed to London, but the Metropolis accorded him the same cold reception that it had done before, and has done since, to others. In 1891 he commenced his famous residence at Malvern, undaunted by the apparently hopeless struggle for recognition, and in 1896, when nearly forty years of age, his now famous cantata, *King Olaf*, consolidated the critics' attentions to his work. In 1900 *Gerontius* was produced and Elgar was made a Doctor of Music by Cambridge. The great oratorio, however, failed to arouse enthusiasm until the news was received in December, 1901, of its remarkable success in Germany. The work retained its popularity in Germany and soon was heard in other countries.

The remarkable speech on *Gerontius* by Richard
Strauss, the German contemporary of Elgar, did
much to open the eyes of doubters, more especially
as the English composer's genius took quite a different
path to that of Strauss. At the present day each
has reached the very height of their conflicting ideals,
and each can testify to the fact that to attain fame
of any real merit means a fight against public prejudice and mental blindness of the most stubborn
type.

Elgar's return to London was a very different thing
to his first acquaintances with the Capital, for it
resulted in a fine, artistic mansion in Hampstead.
" Severn House " is situated in Netherhall Gardens,
which turns off Finchley Road, opposite the Under-
ground Railway Station.

With the memorable production, in 1908, of the
first symphony, Elgar took his place as a great symphonic master, and after the completion of the violin
concerto in 1910, and the E flat Symphony in 1911,
the composer was given an addition to his knighthood
of 1904 in the form of the Order of Merit. This
order is one of the few of any meritorious value, its
members being limited to twenty-four in number
and comprising the most eminent men in Art, Science,
Literature or War. From this period onwards,
Elgar went on working out his ideal and proving
the greatness of his genius. It is not necessary here
to landmark further successes, as the full history of

Elgar's development can be traced in our reviews of his works, which are treated in practically chronological order. Our subject has been to show, through his earlier experiences, the type of man Elgar was in his struggle for recognition, the magnitude of which can only be realised by a knowledge of the condition of British composers at the time. The native musician had to fight a worse enemy than ignorance, in the form of prejudice. Nobody believed in the possibility of good British music, still less the probability of a genius amongst them. Sullivan amused them with his comic operas, but his absolute music was ignored, and had he posed as a symphonic writer, he would have been beaten. The little group who stood by Cowen and Stanford were lost in the din of the big drum of convention. Parry attained some measure of success because he posed as an English Bach before the academics. Edward German struggled to fame, which is now turning to neglect, by sheer originality of style. Every honour is due to Cowen and Stanford who worked on against tradition, while Elgar—why, nobody knew him!

At the full maturity of his genius, Elgar was still the same indomitable spirit. His long-delayed success was not made the occasion for a rest, but as the incentive to finer work, and in the later works we find the same spirit of vigour and that tenacious perseverance that animated his youth.

The personality of Elgar is accepted as courteous, kind and very modest. His conversation often referred to anything but music, and on his art he could cover a wild field of discussive matter. He admired Beethoven, Wagner and the musicianship of British orchestral players and choral societies. On the occasions of his public speeches, he showed his strong views on the municipalisation of music and the need for giving good music, and making good listeners instead of tinkerers on the keyboard. The death of his wife in 1920 came as a tragic damper on the gratification for the enormous growth of public appreciation for his big works.

On various occasions the public saw Elgar in the role of conductor, although he never attempted to propaganda his work. His conducting was vividly suggestive of his personal character as expressed in his music. He appeared to be brimming over with that somewhat explosive "nervous vigour," but although his technical knowledge of the orchestra was superb, it cannot be denied that his works sounded better under the batons of Appleby Matthews, Henry J. Wood and Albert Coates, not to mention the supreme authority of his "life-long" admirer and exponent, Landon Ronald. Nevertheless, Elgar's orchestras were always notable for their response and respect for his genius. His tours to Italy and Holland were notable for the perfect understanding he obtained from the big orchestras of these countries.

His choral conducting was very beautiful and at the same time critical, for his advice to remedy the defect of one choir he was conducting was, " Get a new choir." When an orchestra complained about extra instruments being needed for a work, Elgar told them if a piece had parts for forty harps, get forty harps, even if they only had to play three notes.

Altogether, Elgar showed us in himself a great genius and master of music, and also a great man. There is no doubting his tremendous power of self-expression in music and his utter sincerity. His whole outlook is very serious in quality, and perhaps for that reason he is not quickly and easily understood. While the mass of his own countrymen, apart from a group of enthusiasts, are only now awaking to his true significance, it must be remembered with all fairness that it was Germany, with Richard Strauss prominent, that first acclaimed him as a great choral writer, and it was Germany, in the form of Hans Richter, that first acknowledged his greatness as a symphonic master. The work of Richter for Elgar can never be over estimated. He worked unceasingly in the early days to make the *Enigma Variations* known, and his reward came when he received the dedication of the great *A flat Symphony* and produced it in Manchester and London. No composer ever had a more faithful propagandarist than Elgar did in Richter, and that he knew this is shown by the inscription on the title page of the first symphony, " To Hans Richter, Mus. Doc. True Artist and True Friend."

There is one other name that we must esteem as high as Richter's in connection with Elgar, and that is Landon Ronald. Mr. Ronald is probably that greatest exponent of Elgar that has ever lived, up to the present. His work to make Elgar known has been even more untiring that Richter's. His efforts throughout Great Britain have been so persistent that his name has become almost a synonym of Elgar. His most striking achievements include the securing of appreciation of Sunday afternoon audiences at Albert Hall for the symphonies, each of which takes up best part of an hour to play, and his hard fight against an apathetic public to rescue the *E flat Symphony* from oblivion, culminating in the work being described as one of the finest symphonies since Beethoven's day. He has performed the first symphony in Rome and Paris, and given an orchestral concert devoted entirely to Elgar's works at Queen's Hall, London.

The interpretations by Landon Ronald of Elgar are remarkable for their insight and wealth of expression, and are generally accepted to be the most authoritative. The full extent of the famous conductor's work to make the British public understand the genius in their midst, we are expressly forbidden to mention, but should the facts ever come to light, the world will see yet another example of the self-sacrificing love of true genius for fellow genius.

We are accustomed, rightly enough, to admire the monumental creations of music written in the nineteenth century, but with the equally monumental works of Scriabin, Elgar and Richard Strauss, has not the twentieth made a start that promises to excel its predecessor ?

THE MUSIC

ANALYTICAL AND DESCRIPTIVE NOTES ON ELGAR'S WORKS

FROM OPUS I TO THE LAST, INCLUDING THOSE WITHOUT OPUS NUMBER

OPUS 1. ROMANCE IN E MINOR, FOR VIOLIN AND ORCHESTRA

This little work is immensely interesting, not only for its position in the list of Elgar's works, but for its fresh and melodious character. There is evidence of the now familiar seriousness with which the composer regarded his art ; at the seventh bar we even find a phrase that is quite characteristic of him.

The piece is well written, the violin being treated with much sympathy and insight, signficant perhaps of the future fame and greatness of the *violin concerto* (Op. 61) and *violin sonata* (Op. 82).

For convenience, the *Romance* is almost always played in its arrangement for violin and pianoforte.

OPUS 1a. SUITE No. 1 FOR ORCHESTRA, "THE WAND OF YOUTH." MUSIC TO A CHILD'S PLAY.

First Produced on December 14th, 1907, at a Queen's Hall (London) Symphony Concert.

Dedicated to C. Lee Williams.

The *Wand of Youth* Suites are two in number. The music dates back to 1869, when the composer was only twelve years of age, and was designed to accompany an " unacted play " performed by members of the Elgar family. Edward was also part-author and for several years the play received additions. After a time, he has told us, " the circumstances which gave rise to the little allegory set forth in the play passed away, and with that the play also disappeared."

The music, however, remained in the composer's keeping. Some numbers were completed, but others were only existent in sketches, and Elgar himself testified how delightful it was to go over the youthful efforts and revise them :—" During an enforced rest from larger and more complicated work, it has been an amusement to reconstruct and rehabilitate these pieces . . . " The composer also assured us that although the " orchestration was revised, and some of the movements rewritten, the main features remain as in the original."

The two suites are indicative of a prodigy who remained for many years unknown. They afford the listener a delightful contrast to the composer's greater works, breathing throughout an indescribable freshness and spring-like charm. The decision of Elgar in giving these early efforts to the world, was a happy one, more especially as they are combined with the beauty of his maturity.

The first suite is the more interesting of the two, although the second has its own particular merits.

1. *Overture* (*Allegro molto*). The miniature overture is written in an imposing style. From the first bar it is typically Elgarian in its vigour, and the broad, dignified melody entering at bar nine increases the originality. The number is exhilarating throughout and finely scored.

2. *Serenade* (*Andantino*) .This is one of the lovely little gems that Elgar often wrote down to provide contrast. Throughout it is contemplative and its middle section is a fragment of deep and beautiful inspiration.

3. *Minuet* (*Old Style*) (*Andante*). The minuet has quite an old-world charm and might have been written by Bach for a modern orchestra. It has the welcome flow of parts and is altogether fresh and pleasing.

4. *Sun Dance* (*Presto*). This number is remarkable for its brilliant scoring. Excepting the cantabile section, it seems to merely skim over the different instruments. It is undoubtedly one of the most

fanciful and ingenious little pieces Elgar ever wrote.

5. *Fairy Pipers* (*Allegretto*). The mood of this number throughout is one of idyllic contemplation. The first theme is in thirds and has a gently rocking accompaniment. It is followed by another melody, given out *ppp*, *dolciss*. This second theme is very beautiful and was used again in the Fantasy, *The Starlight Express* (Op. 78).

6. *Slumber Scene* (*Moderato*). The *Slumber Scene* is perhaps the most beautiful number in both suites. Its expression, although simple, comes straight from the soul and makes an irresistible appeal by its human note. The whole atmosphere is wrapped in peaceful contemplation, but a feature of this number is its noble climax, which is undoubtedly a fragment of the greater Elgar.

7. *Fairies and Giants* (*Presto*). This opens with a vigorous but light theme in the lower strings. The subtle idea is continued with melodious harmonies until a magnificent new theme enters. This, from its strength and ponderous attitude, may obviously be the giant's theme. It is repeated with great power, the loud detonations from the bass drum adding to the general heavy splendour. The two themes are worked through again and the movement ends in a brilliant and effective manner.

In point of orchestral power and colour this number is perhaps the most striking in the suite. It is certainly the most exhilarating.

OPUS 1b. SUITE No. 2 FOR ORCHESTRA,
" THE WAND OF YOUTH." MUSIC TO A
CHILD'S PLAY.

First Produced in 1908, at the Worcester Musical
Festival.

Dedicated to Herbert A. Leicester, Mayor of Worcester
(1908).

The second *Wand of Youth* suite is fresh and exceedingly youthful, comprising some of Elgar's most sprightly music.

1. *March* (*Alla marcia. Allegro moderato*). The march opens *pianissimo* and, despite its gracefulness, has a curiously reflective air. The enigmatic Elgar appears to dominate even in the animated middle section, and we may discern, in its infancy, the half-sad and subdued thoughts so often found in the greater works. Altogether the march is exceedingly interesting and suggestive of unseen reflections.

2. *The Little Bells* (*Scherzino*) (*Allegro molto*). This number has opportunities for charming orchestral colour and much use is made of them. The music is exceedingly fluent until we come to the middle section. This consists of a contrasting and expressive theme, foreshadowing vividly the later Elgar. The beautiful melody was used again in the Fantasy, *The Starlight Express* (Op. 78).

3. *Moths and Butterflies* (*Dance*) (*Allegretto*). The orchestration of this piece is brilliant and charming, particularly in the treatment of the wood wind. The opening theme is elusive and it is only when we arrive at the middle one (*grasioso*) that the music becomes sustained. This second theme is, however, exceedingly dainty and trips along with dance-like rhythm.

4. *Fountain Dance* (*Allegretto comodo*). In this number we again come upon exquisite orchestral colouring. The gently rocking bass gives added charm to the fountain-like arpeggio figures constituting the first theme. A second idea is equally rippling in character and the piece ends, or rather falls, like the water from the fountain, to a gentle impression.

5. *The Tame Bear* (*Allegro moderato*). The movement opens with a quaint theme, the uniform rhythm being suggestive of the bear's rolling gait. In the repetition the tambourine is heard, and thus still further is the once familiar street scene suggested. After a time the music is rather subdued ; in fact, the general air of the piece is rather mournful. In all probability the youthful composer felt compassion for the unfortunate animal, deprived of its natural life and haunts.

6. *The Wild Bears* (*Presto*). This number opens with a vigorous theme and throughout is animated and brilliantly scored. The music becomes very forcible and concludes in a magnificent , grandiose manner. The large orchestra and the way it is

treated is indicative of a re-scoring ; the percussion alone includes the bass-drum, cymbals, triangle, side-drum, tambourine and xylophone.

OPUS 2. MOTETS. 1. AVE VERUM. 2. AVE MARIA. 3. AVE MARIS STELLA.

The note of sincerity is significantly struck in these early efforts, which are in places quite profound in sentiment. The motets give the first practical indication of the composer's love for deeply religious choral writing. There are three anthems adapted from them :—1. *Jesu, Word of God incarnate.* 2. *Jesu, Lord of Life and Glory.* 3. *Jesu, Meek and Lowly.*

OPUS 3. ALLEGRETTO IN C MAJOR, FOR VIOLIN AND PIANOFORTE.

Dedicated to The Misses Gedge.

The theme of this little piece is composed of the letters, in their correct order, of the ladies' name. With a fair amount of skill, the composer contrives to keep the idea continually to the fore in a manner that is interesting both to the ear and the eye. It may be instructive to students to follow the theme through its varied course, but it is rather apt to engross too much of the attention. The idea is a little too obvious.

OPUS 4. THREE PIECES, FOR VIOLIN AND PIANOFORTE

There is nothing particularly striking about these pieces, although there are distinct signs of individual style.

OPUS 5. TWO SONGS.

The first published attempt at song-writing is interesting. There is evident seriousness in the conception, which is in itself a merit, when it is considered that trivial writing in this branch of music is often profitable to an unknown writer. We do not believe, however, that Elgar ever intended merely to catch the public ear; his works have done so on their merit alone. The two numbers comprising *Opus* 5, are therefore to be commended to those who would see how a great composer commenced his contributions to the world of song.

OPUS 6. MS.

OPUS 7. SEVILLANA (" SCENE ESPAGNOLE "), FOR ORCHESTRA.

This piece has achieved a certain amount of popularity, being often played by amateurs, and to a lesser

extent, in its arrangement as a piece for violin and
pianoforte. It is not quite so typical as one or two
of its predecessors, but it has considerable warmth
and charm. The attempt at a Southern atmosphere
is original, owing not a little of its success to the
orchestral colouring.

OPUS 8. MS.

OPUS 9. SONATA, FOR VIOLIN AND PIANO-
FORTE. MS.

OPUS 10. THREE PIECES, FOR ORCHESTRA.
No. 1. MAZURKA. No. 2. SERENADE MAUR-
ESQUE. No. 3. CONTRASTS: THE GAVOTTE,
A.D. 1700; THE GAVOTTE, A.D. 1900.

These pieces are of considerable charm, and on the
whole, present an advance on the preceding works.

The *Mazurka* has much grace and charm. The
Serenade was included in Mr. William C. Stockley's
programme at Birmingham in 1883, when the comparatively unknown composer was forced to appear
in response to the applause. The critic of a local
newspaper was surprised to see one so youthful, and
although considering the title as misguiding, gave

the piece a fair measure of praise. It should be remembered that Elgar was then already twenty-five or twenty-six years of age, and was far from anything approaching fame.

Of the two *Gavottes*, the first, in the olden style, is one of the most charming little things Elgar has written. There is a genuine and lovable old-worldness about it, almost approaching the refreshing spirit of the old English dances by Cowen and Edward German.

The modern *Gavotte* is more or less ordinary in style, but forms, as intended, a pleasing contrast to its companion.

OPUS 11. SURSUM CORDA, IN B FLAT, FOR STRINGS, BRASS AND ORGAN.

First Concert Performance in London, September 21st, 1901, at a Queen's Hall Promenade Concert.

To My Friend, H. Dyke Acland, Malvern.

(*Adagio religioso*). This is, by far, the most representative work of Elgar that we have yet discussed. A spirit of lofty ideals and dignity breathes throughout the piece. Even at the present day it is a number that commands a certain respect and admiration. We have noticed in the motet, *Ave Verum*, the composer's regard for religious music ; in the present work he has taken another step towards the great culmination of it, which came with the last three great oratorios.

From the first bars, the *Sursum Corda* has that impressive, grandiose effect, peculiar to the Church music of the Roman Catholics. The middle section contains some very spiritually beautiful harmonies, and altogether, although the piece is not great, we cannot help admiring the seriousness of the writing, both in the æsthetic and the scholastic sense.

OPUS 12. MORCEAU MIGNON, IN E MAJOR, FOR SMALL ORCHESTRA, "SALUT D'AMOUR."

To Carice.

Popularity has come to this piece in a remarkably generous manner. Its undying vogue among all classes has had the effect of making Elgar's name familiar to millions. It is played throughout the the civilised world, and under all sorts of musical conditions. The large symphony orchestra finds it useful, while municipal, cinema and restaurant bands apparently consider it indispensable. Even during the great war, the orchestras at Berlin cinemas never thought of much else but *Salut d'Amour*, for the accompaniment of an amorous scene. The list of arrangements is long, weird, and wonderful ; a full list is given at the end of this account. Despite its popularity, which is quite equal to that of the *Barcarolle* from *Tales of Hofmann* (Offenbach), or Gounod's *Meditation* on the *First Prelude* of Bach, the piece is

C

Sir Edward Elgar

really meritorious. It has a particularly entrancing melody and in places rises to true Elgarian dignity, which imparts it a sense of distinction.

The success of *Salut d'Amour* is gratifying, although we hope, but fear otherwise, that the trifle is not taken by the general public as a representative work of the great composer.

LIST OF ARRANGEMENTS OF *SALUT D'AMOUR*

No. 1 PIANO IN E (Original)
2 PIANO IN B FLAT
3 VIOLIN & PIANO (in E)
4 VIOLIN (Violoncello ad lib. & Piano) (en Ré)
5 TWO VIOLINS & PIANO
6 VIOLONCELLO & PIANO
7 FLUTE & PIANO
8 CLARINET & PIANO
9 OBOE & PIANO
10 SMALL ORCHESTRA (in E) (Original)
11 MANDOLINE & PIANO
12 TWO MANDOLINES & PIANO
13 TWO MANDOLINES & GUITARE
14 ORGAN   (*Lemare*)
15 PIANO FOR 4 HANDS
16 PIANO, VIOLIN & VIOLONCELLO AD LIB.
17 PIANO, 2 VIOLINS & VIOLONCELLO AD LIB.
18 CORNET A PISTONS & PIANO
19 VIOLA & PIANO
20 2 VIOLONCELLI & PIANO

Opus 12

No. 21 PIANO & HARMONIUM
22 ORGAN   (*Grey*)
23 SMALL ORCHESTRA   (*Tourbié*)
24 Guitare
25 FULL ORCHESTRA   (*Kaiser*)

PANSIES:
Vocal Edition by Max Laistner:
The words by Percy Pinkerton

No. 1 IN E FLAT
2 IN F
3 IN G

PANSIES:
VOICE, VIOLIN & PIANOFORTE (in F)
The words by A. C. Bunten

WOO THOU, SWEET MUSIC:

No. 1 IN G
2 IN F
3 IN A
4 IN E FLAT

PENSEES:
French words by G. Ferrari

No. 1 IN G
2 IN F

VIOLA DEL PENSIERO:
Parole di F. Rizzelli

No. 1 IN SOL

LIEBESGRUSS:

Deutsche Uebersetzung von E. Klingenfeld

No. 1 G-DUR

    2 F-DUR

OPUS 13. TWO PIECES FOR VIOLIN AND PIANOFORTE.

The *Salut d'Amour* was followed by another piece of the same type but inferior in general interest, entitled *Mot d'Amour* (an *Intermezzo*). We do not know whether Elgar was under any amorous influence at this time, but both pieces betray a curious earnestness to outline their subject.

Mot d'Amour is No. 1 of Op. 13. It is very frail and contemplative, but not so interesting as the popular preceding piece. It has, however, a truly impressive, almost passionate passage marked *Largamente*, finer than anything in *Salut d'Amour*.

OPUS 14. TWELVE VOLUNTARIES, FOR ORGAN.

These pieces are well-written, and are obviously by one who has a working knowledge of the " King of Instruments." Organists would do well to play them in place of some of the horrible things so often given us.

Elgar sold the set to a publisher for five pounds.

OPUS 15. TWO PIECES, FOR VIOLIN AND PIANOFORTE. No. 1. CHANSON DE NUIT IN G MAJOR. No. 2. CHANSON DE MATIN IN G MAJOR.

First London Orchestral Performance, September 14th, 1901, Queen's Hall Promenade Concert.

There is much personal charm in both these little pieces. The first is unmistakably Elgarian ; an extremely typical phrase occurs at bars seven and eight which is well worthy of digestion by the Elgar student. The piece has considerable expressiveness, and possesses that stirling quality of being direct, but unassuming. The suggestion of the title is faithfully carried out.

The second piece is an exceedingly pleasant contrast to its companion. In place of the subdued nocturnal character, we have the freshness and brightness of the morn. The feeling of this piece may not be so deep as that of the first one, but occasion does not demand it ; in its own particular sphere it is as meritorious as could be wished.

In their orchestral and pianoforte solo garb, the two pieces are equally charming and often played. In the latter arrangement, *Chanson de Matin* was included in the Senior Examination List of Trinity College of Music, London. This is an evident indication of the possibilities and demands the number has for an artistic performance.

OPUS 16. THREE SONGS.

These are original and pleasing in general style, but not directly striking in quality. There is still, however, a conscientious resolution to keep a refined taste, which is worthy of commendation.

OPUS 17. "LA CAPRICIEUSE," FOR VIOLIN AND PIANOFORTE.

An attempt at brilliance is made here, but the piece is in consequence rather inclined to the showy, salon manner. Happily, Elgar never ventured any farther in this style of writing. The piece has often been played by great *virtuosi*, and gramophone records of it are obtainable.

OPUS 18. TWO PART-SONGS.
No. 1. "O HAPPY EYES. No. 2. "LOVE."

Elgar attained a fine reputation as a writer of part-songs, particularly among choral societies in the Midlands and North of England. The two comprising Opus 18, which were published a good many years after their composition, are therefore of certain interest.

In both of them we find a striving after true expression—the aim that the composer always gave first place. The sincerity with which he regards the somewhat romantic character of the verses, is worthy of a tribute. The part-writing is skilfully done, foreshadowing future accomplishments. Altogether, we recommend these two part-songs with confidence to amateur choirs; there is nothing to disappoint and much to please, not to mention the scope for expressive feeling.

OPUS 19. CONCERT-OVERTURE, FOR ORCHESTRA, " FROISSART."

First Produced at the Worcester Musical Festival of 1890.

" . . . When Chivalry
Lifted up her lance on high." (Keats).

This is the first really great work of Elgar, being the commencement of his career as a great symphonic composer, although not yet as a famous one. When we look at the small works that went before it, the overture is a wonderful composition. Its power is undoubted, and the plan and orchestration are conceived in a masterful manner. It is curious that the work did not bring the composer early recognition, but the *Times'* critic of the period could only scoff at Elgar's use of the *Contrafagotto*. Still more curious is it that at the present day, when Elgar's fame is so firmly and widely established, the work continues to remain on the shelf. It does not suffer from excessive length, the financial outlay is not overwhelming, and as these are the general excuses put forward for the neglect of certain other of Elgar's large works, we cannot explain the apparent ignorance of orchestral societies with regard to this early overture.

The inspiration of the work sprung from a scene in *Old Mortality*, by Sir Walter Scott, in which Claverhouse enquires of Morton whether he has ever read the historian, Froissart. On Morton's asserting his ignorance of the man, Claverhouse begins one of the most inspiring rhapsodies that Scott ever wrote :—

Claverhouse : " I have half a mind to contrive you should have six months' imprisonment in order to procure you that pleasure. His chapters inspire me with more enthusiasm than poetry itself. And the noble canon—with what true chivalrous feeling he confines his beautiful expressions of sorrow to the death of the gallant and high-bred knight, of whom it was a pity to see the fall, such was his loyalty to his king, pure faith to his religion, hardihood towards his enemy, and fidelity to his lady-love !— Ah, benedicite ! how he will mourn over the fall of such a pearl of knighthood, be it on the side he happens to favour, or the other. But, truly, for sweeping from the face of the earth some few hundreds of villain churls, who are born but to plough it, the high-born and inquisitive historian has marvellous little sympathy—as little, or less, perhaps, than John Graham of Claverhouse."

The fine passage easily explains Elgar's enthusiasm and the noble character of his overture.

The work opens *Allegro moderato (brillante)*. The whole atmosphere is at once fiery and romantic, often quite Beethovenish. The music soon dies away to *pianissimo*, and then a proud and dignified theme enters. It is thoroughly typical of Elgar, and might well have been inspired by the mental picture of some noble gentleman-at-arms :—

A notable passage for the horns is heard, and immediately leads into another and more contemplative
theme.

The transitional matter, in which the romantic
horn call is heard leads us to the brilliant main
theme :—

After this has been dwelt upon, the knightly theme
rings out in the full orchestra, and the horn call is
again heard. The music now proceeds along in a
magnificent manner, until a sense of quietude comes
over the whole.

The culmination of this is the sweet and gentle
second subject :—

In all its fuller repetitions the peaceful and contem-

plative air is retained ; it might almost represent
the feminine portion of ancient chivalry.

The development section begins with a reminiscence
of the knightly theme, given out by the trombones,
with a *pianissimo* accompaniment. This is immediately answered by the violas with a fragment of the
second subject.

After a time, the music again proceeds with much
gusto and magnificence ; the horn-call appears in full
orchestral form and the *cantabile* theme has a *Con
fuoco* version. Various little effects are heard until
a stirring *crescendo* passage brings us to the re-capit-
ulation. This opens with the main melody, which
is afterwards followed by the quiet theme, heard **at**
first softly, but soon in an imposing fulness. The
horn-call now appears in a mysterious fashion, very
subdued, but with great deliberation, giving an effect
of impressive gravity.

The ensuing *coda* is of great brilliance, the bold
opening matter is much in evidence and the overture
ultimately ends in a grand and imposing manner.
There are many beautiful passages in the *Froissart
Overture* that are not touched upon in the bare analysis, and we cannot help again commenting upon the
fine spirit of the work, together with its wealth of
orchestral colouring. Even at the present day, in the
light of Elgar's greater works, it is a wholesome and
refreshing study, thoroughly worthy of the quotation
from Keats' noble poem.

OPUS 20. SERENADE, FOR STRING
ORCHESTRA.

1. ALLEGRO PIACEVOLE.
2. ANDANTE (LARGHETTO).
3. ALLEGRETTO.

The lovely *String Serenade* holds its popularity to
this day, despite many superior works of the same
type by the composer.

Its chief charm lies in its unassuming loveliness ;
it has the bloom and innocence of youth, a pretty
comparison with its more intricate and deeper followers. The composer made a happy return to the
style of the early *Serenade*, in his lovely string quartet
(Op. 83), especially in the *piacevole* movement, which,
like the slow one of the present work, is the gem of
the piece.

The opening *Allegro* has a graceful mobility, which
is contrasted by the middle portion. The movement,
as a whole, shows a nice sense of phrasing and natural-
ness, although Elgar does not appear to seek for any
special effect, and the simplicity remains unaffected
by a clever use of his slight material.

The slow movement contains, in the main melody,
some of the most beautiful and expressive music the
composer has ever written. The appeal is deep and
human, and we may believe that we have seen, as

often happens in the early works of great composers, a glimpse of the hidden genius, preparing for its inevitable full appearance.

The final movement is in a time afterwards much favoured by the composer—the swinging rhythm of 12-8. The sentiment is not so fine as in the preceding movements, but is pleasant, and maintains the unassuming character of the whole.

We have spoken highly of the *String Serenade*, but it is fully deserving of the praise bestowed upon it, and it is to be regretted that so striking and original an effort is so seldom played, except by Landon Ronald, and a number of amateur string bands.

OPUS 21. MINUET, FOR SMALL ORCHESTRA.

Dedicated to Paul Kilburn.

The style of the *Minuet* is usually dainty, but Elgar has apparently considered it insufficiently so, for his example here is considered to be one of the daintiest in existence. The piece has really no distinctive merit ; its excessive " daintiness " soon becomes rather uninteresting, and we really cannot discern any particular charm anywhere, except in the *Trio* portion. The *Minuet*, however, is neatly written and charmingly scored.

OPUS 22.   SIX VERY EASY EXERCISES
IN THE FIRST POSITION FOR VIOLIN,
WITH PIANOFORTE ACCOMPANIMENT.

These studies are fresh and interesting, and combine this with certain technical objects. They are
extremely useful as an addition to the violin school,
although it would be interesting to know what
prompted the composer to write them.

OPUS 23. PART-SONG, WITH ORCHESTRAL
ACCOMPANIMENT;   SPANISH   SERENADE,
(" STARS OF THE SUMMER NIGHT ").

Words by Longfellow.

The setting to these verses from the famous poet's
Spanish Student, is effectively done. The music is
always pleasing, and has some touches of southern
warmth and romanticism. It is strange that the
arch-programmist, Ernest Newman, finds it hard to
imagine the Spanish atmosphere. How, therefore,
is the ordinary person, who only loves music for its
own sake, to appreciate the work ? Yet we apparently
can do so, for the *Spanish Serenade* appeals to us as
pure music.

OPUS 24. FIVE ETUDES CARACTERISTIQUES,
         FOR   VIOLIN.

In this further attempt by Elgar in the world of
studies, we find a more advanced technical aim.
The pieces are original and, like the set comprising
Op. 22, combine the mechanical object with a sense
of melody, generally pleasing to the ear.

OPUS 25. SYMPHONY FOR CHORUS AND
       ORCHESTRA, " THE BLACK KNIGHT,"
              (*DER SCHWARZE RITTER*).

The Poem by Uhland, Translated by Longfellow.

This is the most important of all Elgar's works
up to this period. There can be no mistaking in it
his real talent and enthusiasm for dramatic subjects,
a force that wields considerable power in his greater-
choral works.

The scene opens with the celebration, by an aged
king, of *Pentecost, the Feast of Gladness*. His son has
been successful in vanquishing all who opposed him,
at the tournament. His victories receive a check,
however, by an unknown knight in black, who un-
horses him.

The scene now changes to the hall, where the company are dancing. The mysterious knight enters

and dances with the king's daughter, with disastrous
results, for :—

" . . . From breast and hair
   Down fall from her the fair
   Flowerets, faded, to the ground . . . "

The banquet is held, but the old king is troubled by
the pale faces of his children. Seeing this, the " grim
guest " hands them a beaker of wine, telling them of
its supposed restorative powers. They drink, and
before the eyes of their terrified father, grow still more
ghastly and die. The king appeals to the Black
Knight to take him as well, but the strange figure
only replies :—

" Roses in the spring I gather."

The whole spirit of the work is vividly portrayed
by the composer. We hear the clamour of the tournament, the gracefulness of the dance, the banquet,
all in realistic and contrasting effects.

The most striking character is that of the Black
Knight. A mysterious air always settles over the
music on reference to him, and a sense of foreboding
is sometimes so awesome, that the listener instinc-
tively recoils from the thought of the attendant
evil.

The material generally, is handled in a manner that
justifies the title of a *symphony*, although the work is
more often and naturally referred to as a *cantata*.
Altogether we believe the *Black Knight* to be a fine

work, giving evidence of exceptional genius, and in no way influentially overshadowed by the larger works that followed. In the light of later experiences, we still continue to find our interest ensorbed by the understanding with which the composer treated his subject.

OPUS 26. TWO THREE-PART SONGS FOR FEMALE VOICES, WITH ACCOMPANIMENTS FOR TWO VIOLINS AND PIANOFORTE, OR FOR ORCHESTRA.

No. 1. " THE SNOW."
No. 2. " FLY, SINGING BIRD."

Words by C. Alice Elgar.

These two part-songs are, perhaps, as widely known as any of the composer's similar works.

The Snow is very delicately written, and has much sincere feeling, although a little polished, it is true.

Fly, Singing Bird is also elegantly written, but is more poetical and somewhat impassioned in feeling.

The impression left upon us by these songs, in the light of the preceding works is that of progress ; there is a certain obviousness that Elgar was already becoming a composer of a high order, and with a distinctive style.

The poetry, which is by Lady Elgar, is of a refined order.

OPUS 27. CHORAL SUITE, FOR CHORUS AND ORCHESTRA, "FROM THE BAVARIAN HIGHLANDS."

This suite was published in 1896, and was the remembrance of a summer holiday spent at Garmisch. The words are " imitated from Bavarian Volkslieder and Schnadahüpfler." The songs are of a pleasant and homely character, and fortunately exist in a form that has pianoforte accompaniment. By this time we have seen Elgar's preference for orchestral colouring, but it is not always wise for new composers to write in such a large manner, as chances of performance are rare. Almost all the songs that have become popular have had to be arranged with the accompaniment for pianoforte, if this instrument was not the original one written for.

The first number in this suite is entitled *The Dance* (*Sonnenbichl*) and is exceedingly pretty and refreshing. The variety is of the most wholesome type and thoroughly captivating.

No. 2. *False Love* (*Wamberg*) is also pretty, and deals with a jilted lover. Some attempt at pathos is made, but the atmosphere of the other songs is too pleasing to escape from and the result is therefore not as evidently intended.

The third number is a *Lullaby* (*In Hammersbach*),

and is the most beautiful of the series. The pleasant German country dance and the contrasting section cannot be aptly described. The song is simple and tender, but there is much evidence of the deeper Elgar, which accounts for the personal appeal it makes to the listener.

The fourth song, *Aspiration (Bei Sankt Anton)* is short and has a hymn-like character. It is a welcome idea between its contrasting neighbours and we should not deem it the least important of the suite.

No. 5, the country love song is entitled *On the Alp (Hoch Alp)*. It is very simple in construction, but has a really becoming charm, particularly in the ever effective, when discreetly used, "Ah," sung by the female voices.

The last of the set is *The Marksmen (Bei Murnau)*. This the most exhilarating of all. The excitement of the village over the shooting-match, is at once conveyed by the bustling character of the opening theme. This is brilliantly treated until a solemn and broad melody is heard. The new theme is in the magnificent style of the serious Elgar and its grandiose version, as an orchestral piece, is in itself inspiring. It is a fine contrast to the boisterous animation of the opening theme.

OPUS 27. THREE BAVARIAN DANCES, FOR
ORCHESTRA.

First London Performance, October 11th, 1898, at a
Queen's Hall Promenade Concert.

These are an orchestral adaptation of three numbers
from the choral suite, *From the Bavarian Highlands*,
and were published in 1897.   They are also available
as a pianoforte solo and for violin and pianoforte.

The dances have meritoriously attained considerable popularity, being better known than the choral
suite itself.   The numbers comprising the version
are :—No. 1. *The Dance.*   No. 3. *Lullaby.*   No. 6.
The Marksmen.

OPUS 28.   SONATA IN G, FOR ORGAN.

1. ALLEGRO MAESTOSO. 2. ALLEGRETTO.
3. ANDANTE ESPRESSIVO. 4. FINALE PRESTO.

Composed for the Visit of some American Musicians
to Worcester Cathedral in 1898.

The *Organ Sonata* of Elgar is at once a grand and
noble work.   It abounds in originality, is inseparably
connected with its instrument and full of poetical
fire.   It is truly a work that any composer could be
proud of, particularly when it stands as the sole

representative of his work in this sphere. (Elgar's other works for the organ being of small dimensions).

1. The first movement is notable for the striking qualities of its themes. The structural idea is not so fine as that of certain other masters, but we may overlook this on the grounds of it being still early work of a slow developing type of genius. The *Allegro* invariably makes a lasting impression on the intelligent listener.

2. The *Allegretto* is written in an independent manner, the composer allowing his fancy considerable relaxation. There is much that pleases the ear and confirms the excellent impression made by the opening movement.

3. The slow movement is founded on a broad and noble melody. Throughout, there is a sincerity and loftiness of ideal that makes it something more than a formal inclusion. Like Beethoven, Elgar always found the slow movement a medium for the expression of his most beautiful thoughts. The present example is interesting for its own sake, as well as being the significant forerunner of well known others.

4. The *Finale* is animated, but possesses much that is melodious. It has a connection with the preceding movement in the form of a reminiscence of the beautiful theme already spoken of.

The *Sonata* is well known, but not often played in its entirety. The reason, perhaps, for this is the presence in places of formidable technical difficulties, but the work will repay any time taken to overcome these obstacles to greater recognition.

Unfortunately, the majority of organists have very little spare time to cultivate technical resources but this makes their well-known achievements all the more honourable.

Published by a German firm, the registration requires considerable adaptation to English and American instruments.

OPUS 29. ORATORIO, "THE LIGHT OF LIFE" (LUX CHRISTI). SOLI FOR SOPRANO, CONTRALTO, TENOR AND BARITONE.

Produced at the Worcester Musical Festival of 1896

Words Written and Arranged by the Rev. E. Capel-Cure.

This was Elgar's first choral work to be written for a festival, and, according to himself, the last, for he deprecated the idea of a composer having to write to order.

The work is in the usual English style, with certain personal touches of the composer. The *libretto* is partly original and partly arranged from the Scriptures, or Holy Scriptures as Elgar would prefer it.

A *prelude* for the orchestra, entitled *Meditation,*

commences the oratorio. It begins with a solemn theme and its supplement, the motives of the blind man and his longing for light. (It is on this and the miracle of Jesus in healing him, that the work is constructed). Another spiritual theme appears and leads into a more important one, this being the motive of Jesus, the Giver of Light.

The vocal work begins with a chorus of Levites singing in praise of the Lord, and after a time the blind man is heard praying for light. Following repetitions of these sections, is the approach of Jesus, who is asked by his disciples the reason of the man's affliction. A beautiful solo is now given to the blind man's mother, who also asks the reason of her son's blindness. Jesus answers in a calm and Divine manner. It is doubtful whether anything more beautiful could be imagined, than the expression Elgar always gives to our Lord ; in just such peaceful, soothing strains as these, we imagine, would the voice of Jesus sound. This impression is given us in the later oratorios, *The Apostles* and *The Kingdom*, and the reader's pardon is asked for if attention is again drawn to it in these works. It is an insight to the composer's deeper religious feelings.

Jesus performs the miracle, and the man's solo of gratitude contains some of the most human music in the oratorio. After this the Pharisees and the people are heard contending as to whether Jesus is a sinner or of God. The mother of the man testifies

to the miracle, but after further discussion the man
is cast out, and the mother and female chorus invoke
woe on the shepherds of the flock.

Jesus seeks for the man, and on finding him, receives
an assertion of his good faith and then has a fine solo,
I am the Good Shepherd. A chorus, praising Him as
the " Light of the World " brings this scholarly and
beautiful work to a finish.

OPUS 30. CANTATA, " SCENES FROM THE
SAGA OF KING OLAF."

Produced at the North Staffordshire Musical Festival,
held at Hanley, 1896.

The Poem by Longfellow, with Additions by H. A.
Acworth.

The Light of Life had caused the critics to keep a
watchful eye on Elgar and his next work was awaited
with more than ordinary interest.   The magnificence
of *King Olaf*, however, surprised even the most
optimistic. The *cantata* is remarkable both for its
beauty and the dramatic power of its characters.
In this statement we do not give a thought to the
libretto, which is rather inconsistent in places, but
the strength of Elgar's characters seems to impart new
life and interest to the whole story, or rather legend.

The composer himself has told us how to regard

the *cantata*, in the following words :—In the following scenes it is intended that the performers should be looked upon as a gathering of skalds* ; all, in turn, take part in the narration of the saga, and occasionally, at the more dramatic points, personify for the moment some important character." The whole text of the scenes is founded on a collection of sagas of the Norwegian kings, entitled *Heimskringla*, by Snorre Sturlesson, an Icelander who lived in the twelfth century.

The work commences with five bars of an enigmatic and somewhat moody theme, intended to be the motive of the ancient tales.

This is immediately followed by the chorus, who commence to tell of this wonderful old book. From the commencement, the atmosphere is strangely romantic and appropriate. A *recitative* calls upon Thor, the God of Thunder, who is symbolised with a passage of great power, thundered out by chorus and orchestra :—

I am the God Thor I am the

War God. I am the Thun___der___er

*Bards.

Another powerful theme is also alloted him :—

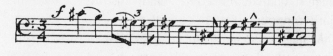

His long oration is in the nature of a challenge, which is rather boastful, as the following lines from it will show :—

> " The light thou beholdest
> Stream from the heavens,
> In flashes of crimson,
> Is but my red beard,
> Blown by the night-wind,
> Affrighting the nations.

> " Jove is my brother ;
> Mine eyes are the lightning ;
> The wheels of my chariot
> Roll in the thunder.
> The blows of my hammer
> Ring in the earthquake !

> " Force rules the world still.
> Has ruled it, shall rule it ;
> Meekness is weakness,
> Strength is triumphant,
> Over the whole earth
> Still is it Thor's-Day."

The Galilean God, however, defies Thor, and a challenge to combat rings out. Olaf sails into Drontheim fjord to accept it.

A lengthy tenor solo of great beauty, tells the history of Olaf. Although born in exile, he is the rightful heir to his father's kingdom ; his desire is to avenge his parents and promote the Christian faith in his country. The saga itself fully describes the life of Olaf. His voyage, the thoughts of his mother and his recallings of many contests with the fierce sea-kings are graphically portrayed in the music.

The chorus tell in unison of the landing of Olaf and his men. Ironbeard, a pagan chieftain meets them and defies the offer of Christianity. Olaf smashes the images of Thor with his axe, and Ironbeard springs forward in a rage. He is shot by one of Olaf's men, but refuses in death to forsake his gods. An admirable action, however mistaken, and the burden of the poignant solo :—

IRONBEARD.

" All-Father, I come ! true to honour and troth,
To the faith of my fathers, and Odin the Goth.
O wide should the doors of Valhalla unroll
For a hero who gives for it body and soul.
King Olaf the Norseman ! perchance it shall be,
That thy Peace-God may rule o'er the Norlander free ;
But with axe in his hand, and with sword upon thigh,
And his face to his slayer doth Ironbeard die."

The men of Drontheim are converted, this being told in an effective manner by the chorus.

As compensation for Ironbeard's death Olaf weds the chieftain's daughter. She sings, however, of revenge and on the bridal night approaches the sleeping Olaf with murderous intentions, the orchestra giving a realistic impression of the scene. The young warrior awakes, however, and sees the dagger gleaming in the air.

In the ensuing duet, Gudrun has evidently attempted to camouflage the dagger as a bodkin for her hair, but Olaf denounces her. At dawn she rides away, disappearing from his life for ever. This scene concludes with a muted trumpet call and a few lines by the chorus.

The next scene describes the appearance of " The Wraith of Odin," the pagan god, the bards being occupied with a long story of how the spirit appeared. Olaf and his guests were at the feast, when the door opens and a mysterious one-eyed figure appears, wrapped in a hooded cloak. The chorus tell in impressive strains of the acceptance of ale, and the telling of old sagas.

Olaf falls asleep, and on his awakening in the morning, can find no trace of his mysterious guest, although all the doors are barred and the watch dogs undisturbed. He concludes that the death of Odin indicates the triumph of the Christian faith, and the hymn heard at the conversion of the men of Drontheim is now repeated.

A heathen queen, Sigrid by name, now appears and Olaf desires her hand in marriage, and also conversion to Christianity. She refuses, and as in the case of Ironbeard, Olaf takes strong measures. He declares his readiness to give "body and soul to flame" before he would marry her, a heathen, and informs her of her lack of beauty and youth, concluding by striking her in the face with his glove. All this is told in a very effective manner, the ensuing vow of revenge by the queen being especially dramatic.

The king is more successful with the next lady, Thyri, who seeks protection from the old ruler, Burislaf of Wenland, who wishes to marry her. Olaf weds her in face of the future, the troubles of which are emphatically told by the chorus :—

> " For surely, if here she remain,
>   It is war with King Svend the Dane,
>   And King Burislaf the Wend."

The whole of the writing around this section is obviously the work of a great master.

Olaf promises to win back the lands and happiness of his queen. We next hear Sigrid, the malicious, who has married the king Svend, persuading her husband to attack Olaf. A passionate outburst of her hate is finely portrayed in a passage for the trombones.

The horns and trumpets ring out a brazen challenge

to the Dane, who has sailed against Olaf, the chorus having told of his prowess. In the battle Olaf is defeated, and the insidious motive of Sigrid is significantly recalled. The solemn tolling of a bell is heard, and the young warrior apparently disappears for ever.

We now come upon the mother of Olaf, praying in a Convent. She hears the voice of St. John, telling of the triumph of Christ over paganism. The chorus quietly sing of the God of Love :—

> " Cross against corslet,
>   Love against hatred,
>   Peace cry for War-cry,"

and soon the tale of tragedy concludes in a quiet tone of resignation, betraying, perhaps, the inner feelings of the composer and certainly those of the listener.

The *cantata* is undoubtedly a masterpiece, for in many places the music rises to heights not surpassed in the composer's later works. We can quite understand the popularity of the work among choral societies, for it is always capable of arousing enthusiasm, both among singers and audience.

OPUS 31. TWO SONGS.

These are of general interest, but not exceptional in their conception. They are, however, well and pleasingly written.

OPUS 32. IMPERIAL MARCH, FOR ORCHESTRA

Composed about 1897.

This march originated at the time of Queen Victoria's Diamond Jubilee. It is very popular in its arrangement for organ, being broad and rich in its harmonies. The work is of a superior type, in comparison with most others in the same category. The pompous swinging tune, together with the quieter middle section and the gorgeous colour of the whole, make it an extremely effective march.

OPUS 33. BALLAD, FOR CHORUS AND ORCHESTRA, "THE BANNER OF ST. GEORGE." SOPRANO SOLO, *Ad Lib.*

Composed about 1897. Words by Shapcott Wensley.

The story is founded upon the familiar legend of St. George of Cappadocia. The town of Sylene is ravaged by a dragon, and the maiden Sabra offers herself as a sacrifice, in order that the town shall be free.

As she is about to meet her death, St. George appears and after a struggle, slays the fiery monster.

The music amply partakes of the patriotic fervour of the verses, and a healthy *epilogue, It Comes from the Misty Ages,* has met with some popularity. The *cantata*, although only in places showing the deeper Elgar, is stirring and representative of the true national spirit, which the composer always admired and felt.

OPUS 34. TE DEUM AND BENEDICTUS IN F.

Composed for the Hereford Festival of Music, 1897.

We believed that this work was written especially for the festival, but many Elgar lovers declare that the composer merely offered what had been in his mind for some time previously.

The setting aroused considerable discussion at the time, the favourite criticism being that it was not church music. Whether this is correct or not, there is no doubt that it is a fine work ; Buckley even says that, " There is no setting of the Ambrosian hymn that can be compared with Elgar's in point of descriptive character." This is very true, but it is also the fact that aroused antagonism. It was not conventional enough.

While fearful of being regarded as conservative in our views, we venture to remark that the setting would be better for a little restraint. There are too many Elgarisms and too little regard for the surroundings which the work will meet with in actual performance. We admire the magnificent shattering

of conventions by the force of human expression in
The Dream of Gerontius, but it is just a little too
premature in this *Te Deum and Benedictus*. Nevertheless, we do not withdraw our opinion that it is a
very fine and worthy work as regards musicianship,
both in brain and heart.

OPUS 35. CANTATA, " CARACTACUS.'
SOPRANO, TENOR, BARITONE & BASS SOLI

Produced in 1898.

Words by H. A. Acworth.

Caractacus is bold and abounding with touches of
the great genius. It is as fine a work as Elgar has
written and with the following one, the *Variations
for Orchestra*, forms an epoch-making event in the
master's career. The expression is unusually deep,
and the writing that of a thorough master of the art.
The whole outlook of the composer appears to be
broadened and approaching the great climax of his
choral writing. Scene 1 is the Camp of the Britons
on the Malverns. It is night and Caractacus and his
army are entering. The chorus of Britons tell of the
Roman invasion and boldly announce their defiance
of the enemy. Caractacus speaks to them and then
goes to the spring of Taranis. At the foot of a mound
he falls into soliloquising ; his past battles come
before him and the future looms up gloomily. After

E

a mental struggle he determines to make one more great attempt to overthrow the Roman menace.

His daughter Eigen and her lover, Orben, a minstrel, now appear, the former telling of the Druids' prophecy of victory if the Britons conduct the fight in the forest. The music is decidedly realistic in its contemplative spirit and the scene closes after the three have discussed the prospective meeting with the priests on the morrow. The sentry-call, *Watchman Alert!* is heard in the distance and the peace of night settles down over all.

The next day the Druids and Druidesses take the omens in the grove of the sacred oak. The music assumes an air of mystery as Orbin is about to read the signs. Foreboding strains describe his perception of the Roman eagle, its beak and talons stained with blood.

The Arch-Druid, however, glibly tells Caractacus, on his arrival, that the omens have foretold victory for the Britons. The famous sword-song and chorus are now heard, which need no description.

Orbin attempts to tell the chieftain the truth, but the Arch-Druid curses him and casts him out. He throws down his harp and goes to prepare for the battle, a vigorous chorus of curses following him.

The next scene is morning in the Severn Forest. The orchestra gives out a *Prelude* which is followed by a chorus of youths and maidens. Eigen enters, and while waiting for her lover, sings a lovely song of

nature. Orbin now appears and tells of his deter-
mination to fight for Caractacus. Intermingled with
the chorus is heard the dialogue between the two.
This is followed by their duet of peace and love, the
music being very calm and natural.

The fourth scene opens with a frightened figure
for the chorus of maidens, who have heard of the
defeat of the Britons. Eigen tells of the Druidess
who cursed Caractacus and foretold his downfall as
he left the forest to fight. The defeated chieftain and
the remnant of his soldiers appear and the sad story
is told in an expressive manner, rising to a long wail
of utter despair.

The next scene opens in a melancholy manner;
Caractacus sees the end of Freedom and the maidens
have a pitiful lament as their countrymen are carried
away to Roman slavery. The whole is accompanied
by a perpetual motion of despair.

Soon the voices are left behind and the iron spirit
of the conquerors is felt. The scene leads without a
break into the next, in which we come upon all the
pompous splendour of ancient Rome.

A gorgeous march is heard, broken once by the
voices of the captives, as the men apparently march
through the city. The cavalcade at last arrives at
the seat of Claudius Cæsar, who commands the
chieftain to kneel for mercy. A noble note is struck
when the Briton refuses and tells of his fight for
freedom, asking why the Romans wish to disturb so

peaceful a nation. He pleads for his brethren at the price of his own life. Eigen and Orbin have a duet in which they dwell on their native land, but refuse to live at their leader's expense. The populace demand the slaying of the captives, but the Emperor declares they shall live in his city in freedom.

A sad quartet follows, describing the Britons' resignation to " our golden chain."

The work ends with the patriots proudly singing of the future might of Briton and the fall of Roman tyranny.

The *Cantata* has not the charm of *King Olaf*, but as we have seen, it is a work of greater aim, which at times makes it appear rather forced. The spirit, however, is always admirable and indicative of greater things to come.

OPUS 36. VARIATIONS ON AN ORIGINAL THEME (" ENIGMA "), FOR ORCHESTRA.

First Appeared at a Concert Conducted by Dr. Hans Richter, M.V.O., at the St. James' Hall, London, on 19th June, 1899.

Dedicated to My Friends Pictured Within.

This is the first great work of Elgar in which his supreme genius was fully manifested. His career as a great master, so often indicated in the preceding works, was now fully evident to the world.

Opus 36

Familiar as we are with works of the same type by the immortal Beethoven, Brahms, Tchaikovsky, Dvorak and others, we have no hesitation in deeming Elgar's *Variations* as the most beautiful in existence. The utter sincerity, the wide contrasts of human character united by one whose sole aim was to make a noble whole, is a personal appeal to all music lovers.

The score of the *Variations* was sent to Richter at Vienna by his London agent. The German at once accepted it on its merits alone, for he had not then become acquainted with the composer. In justice to the conductor, we must say that he was fully aware of Elgar's powers, and always gave his works a prominent place ; in fact he won England for Elgar, as Buckley says, by the *Variations*, in the same way that he won England for Wagner with the *Tannhauser Overture*. An example to some of our own conductors who worship Wagner in a narrow-minded fashion.

It was on the advice of Jaeger (once editor of the *Musical Times*) that Elgar added a *coda* to his work, and also in after years composed his *First Symphony*.

Concerning the *Variations*, the following extract from a letter, written by Elgar in a jocular vein to a friend, is interesting. It appeared in the *Musical Times'* article on Elgar in 1900, copies of which are still happily obtainable, for this number was packed with personal information about the composer.

" . . . As to myself the following are the F A X

about me. Just completed a set of *Symphonic Variations* (theme original) for orchestra—thirteen in number (but I call the *finale* the fourteenth, because of the ill-luck attaching to the number). I have in the *Variations* sketched portraits of my friends—a new idea, I think—that is, in each *Variation* I have looked at the theme through the personality (as it were) of another Johnny. I don't know if 'tis too intimate an idea for print, it's distinctly amusing. . . Other compositions are nebulous at present."*

The above letter, of course, explains the intention of the *Variations*, which are, however, as serious as the letter is humorous.

Each number of the set bears the initials or pseudonym of one of the composer's friends, but it is not intended that the work should be regarded as of a programme character. On this point we admire Newman, an advocate of programme music, who says : " It is not at all necessary to have this key, however, in order to appreciate the work, which may confidently appeal to us as music pure and simple. It is full of delicate fancy and beauty tinged with warm feeling ; and the consummate art of the orchestration makes it a perpetual delight to the ear."

To give a list of the *Variations* entails unnecessary space, so the indication and speed of each one will be given as we proceed.

The Theme. Enigma (Andante) The theme itself

* (Reprinted by courtesy of the *Musical Times*).

Opus 36

is remarkable for its beautiful and somewhat sad expressiveness. The composer himself, in later years, described it as expressing his sense of loneliness as an artist. We give the theme in Elgar's arrangement on two staves:—

VARIATIONS

The meaning of the word " enigma " in connection with the score is, according to the composer, that another and larger theme goes with the one we hear. What this theme is no one but Elgar knew, for it is never heard.

Variation 1.   *C.A.E.* (*L'istesso tempo*).   The initials of this number are obviously those of the composer's wife.   The character of the music is subdued, but very expressive.   It mounts to a noble climax, which is followed by an impressive descent.   Altogether the movement is one that gives food for reflection in a peaceful manner.

Variation 2.   *H.D.S.-P.* (*Allegro*).   This opens with a quaint little semiquaver figure which is continued throughout, even when the first part of the theme rolls broadly along. The effect, or impression, is one of constant chatter.

Variation 3. *R.B.T.* (*Allegretto*). The playful mood is apparent here. There are leaping sixths, big and little runs in triplets. The story is told in a jerky, care-free manner.

Variation 4. *W.M.B.* (*Allegro di molto*). A quick *staccato* version of the first part of the theme is given, followed by a *fortissimo* rendering of the major section. The latter is accompanied by boldly undulating passages for the strings. The *staccato* idea is resumed quietly, but soon the whole works up into a magnificent outburst by the full orchestra, the rhythm being fiercely marked by the drums. The person who inspired this number would appear to be impetuous.

Variation 5. *R.P.A.* (*Moderato*). A graver note is now struck, the theme being commenced by the bassoons and basses against a saddened accompaniment. This is followed by a version of the major section of the theme, given out by the flutes, the oboe having a supporting idea. The violins and oboes immediately follow this with a gay *scherzando*. The opening mood returns, the accompaniment being in the bass and the melody above, the latter played by the higher pitched wood-wind. The *scherzando* figure reappears, but the movement ends in somewhat mournful contemplation. The next number enters without a break.

Variation 6. *Ysobel* (*Andantino*). This is very

short, but possesses a peculiar charm. It is, perhaps, more enigmatic than any of them. Its whole existence is wrapt in sombre contemplation. Even a bar or so of lighter colouring fails to banish the air of sadness, quiet and reflective.

Variation 7. Troyte (Presto). A sharp, arresting figure for the drums opens No. 7. This idea is persistently heard throughout the movement. The time is one semibreve to a bar, a sensible *presto* version of the usual 4-4. The theme is derived from the major portion of the original and is delivered by the woodwind and violas. Each phrase commences softly, rapidly loudening and then softening again. Soon the music works up to a loud passage for trombones, tuba, basses and bassoons, while the strings have rapid and exhilarating flights. The drum figure reappears and in the general excitement, somewhat resembles a cannonade. At the end the downward sweep of the strings is exceedingly dizzy ; the drum is heard at the very last, thus emphasising its highly important role.

The number is a triumph of orchestration, abounding with health and vigour that is delightful to record.

Variation 8. W.N. (Allegretto). The clarinets give out the theme in a version in sixths, the gently flowing rhythm impressing the calmness and contentment of the personage. The strings take up the rhythm, followed presently by little ascending trills for the oboe, working up in half-a-bar from *piano* to a *sforzando*, which is immediately hushed again to *piano*. While the atmosphere of repose continues its course, the bass makes some show of strength, independently, but the complacent air ultimately triumphs, the movement ending in the dominant mood. This number leads without a break into the next.

Variation 9. *" Nimrod "* (*Adagio*). This movement, a tribute to A. J. Jaeger, who did much to make Elgar known, is the most spiritual and lofty of the set. It is said to have been inspired by the beauty of Beethoven's slow movements. The commencement bears the indication, *noblimente*, which afterwards grew to be symbolical of the composer. It became his favourite indication, and throughout his works from now it is used innumerable times.

The noble statement of the theme is repeated with fuller scoring, and the spiritual atmosphere becomes more intense as the music proceeds, the final statement being a direct outburst from the inner feelings of a great soul. The colour is strikingly rich and full, and altogether we do not call to mind many works that have such a wealth of noble and lofty sentiments combined in so short a space. Ernest Newman's regard for this is worthy of attention, his final words on it are to the effect that it breathes an elevated inspiration as great as any modern composer can show.

Variation 10. *Intermezzo, Dorabella* (*Allegretto*). This exquisite number is often played, and is published, as a separate piece. It is of the utmost daintiness, both in character and orchestration. Snatches of a little melody are given out by the woodwind, accompanied in a fluttering manner by the muted strings. The middle section, in G minor, is exceedingly graceful. The opening theme returns and is followed by the middle section, now transposed into its tonic major. The *Variation* ends with a few references to the dainty opening idea.

Variation 11. *G.R.S.* (*Allegro di molto*). The characteristics of this number are fire and giant-like humour. The strings sweep down through three octaves, and bassoons and basses give out a *staccato* version of the opening section of the theme. This is followed by the wood-wind and violins giving out the second section with a rapid chromatic accompaniment. This is stated in a fuller form and presently the brass gives out a jerky version of the first section. The wildness is resumed and concludes with a brilliant ascending *arpeggio* passage.

Variation 12. *B.G.N.* (*Andante*). The lovely melody for the 'cellos is a notable feature of this *Variation*. It is sometimes acclaimed the most beautiful of the series, if number nine is deemed the most noble.

It commences with two expressive bars for solo 'cello, derived from the opening of the original theme, and the instrument now embarks *pianissimo* on its expressive and penetrating flow of melody. The middle section is suggestive of the minor part of the theme, and a noble climax is heard. A repetition of the two opening bars leads us into the next number.

Variation 13.* * * (*Moderato*). The personage of this *Variation* was on a sea voyage at the time of its composition. The clarinet gives out a melody, and has a gently undulating accompaniment in the strings. Soon a *ppp.* figure appears, the effect of which is like the throbbing of the engines of a great liner. The kettle drum gives out a distant roll, and a soft quotation from Mendelssohn's *Calm Sea and a Prosperous Voyage Overture* is heard. The gentle melody continues its peaceful journey, always accompanied by the throbbing idea, which increases in significance until the opening figure returns. The quotation is again heard and gradually the whole fades away, like the gradual vanishing of a ship over the horizon.

Variation 14. *Finale*, E.D.U. (*Allegro*). The great *finale* commences *pianissimo*, swiftly moving in a heroic, martial strain, the *staccato* beats in the accompaniment (on the weaker accents) resounding in a striking manner. The determined stride increases in strength and agility until a grand outburst is reached in a bar marked *largamente*. A brilliant effect is here obtained, as the time changes in the next bar to the original *allegro*, by the sudden and abrupt delivery of the remaining portion of the phrase begun at the end of the *largamente* bar.

Some thunderous passages occur in which the martial element is distinctly prevalent. Soon a quieter section is reached, in which we hear the second part of the original theme. This increases in prominence until we come to a larger version of the *Ninth Variation*, which now has a counter theme both above and below it. The music increases in dignity culminating in a great *stringendo* passage terminating on a triple *sforzando* chord. Only a quaver rest separates this from the *pianissimo* reappearance of the martial strain. Familiar features return, another *sf.* is reached, but soon all becomes hushed and a mysterious passage appears, in the impenetrable mood of the *scherzo* of Beethoven's *C Minor Symphony*. This leads into the tender strains of the *First Variation*, now even more exquisite. The second part of the theme is again heard and soon we reach a great swell leading to the spirit of *Variation* 9. The orchestration grows richer and richer, still loftier does the music become until at last we reach the colossal splendour of the last great *fff.* passage. It is not to be wondered that all the critics and others remark on this wonderful *finale*. At the end of the score the composer has written : " *Bramo assai, poco spero, nulla chieggio* " (*Tasso*).

The *Enigma Variations* of Elgar will always remain a monument of music ; nothing, excepting some of the composer's other works, has surpassed them in loftiness of ideal and sheer personal magnitude.

OPUS 37. A CYCLE OF FIVE SONGS, FOR CONTRALTO, WITH ORCHESTRAL ACCOMPANIMENT, " SEA PICTURES."

Produced in 1899.

This fine collection is the most popular of any of Elgar's attempts as a modern song writer. As sung by Madame Clara Butt, their beauty is remarkable for its contrasting colour and depth of feeling.

No. 1. *Sea Slumber Song.* Words by the Hon. Roden Noel. The first song claims much of our attention in the orchestral accompaniment, which is minutely faithful to the surrounding atmosphere of the words. The mother hushing the wild voices from her child, is accompanied by a mysterious tremor on the drums, a faint clang of the gong, in addition to the *arpeggios* for the harp and the equally mysterious octaves for the strings. Altogether the song is remarkable for its realism.

No 2. *In Haven* (*Capri*). Words by C. Alice Elgar. The charm of this number has made it popular among many hundreds of amateurs. It is not difficult, and the verses are of a refined, poetical order. The utmost complacency prevails throughout and the song always leaves a satisfied effect on the listener.

No. 3. *Sabbath Morning at Sea*, from a poem by Mrs. Browning. The profound and religious Elgar is evident in this number, rising in places to th heights that make his songs far away from the ordinary ballad type. An impressive climax is one of its outstanding features.

No. 4. *Where Corals Lie.* Words by Richard Garnett. This song, like No. 2, enjoys an extensive popularity. The music is fresh and natural, the accompaniment being expressively Elgarian.

No. 5. *The Swimmer*, from a poem by Adam Lindsay Gordon. The last number opens with an orchestral " depiction " of the storm-swept sea. This graphic painting is typical of the entire song, which is notable for its realistic and pictorial character. We believe the dramatic intensity, faithfully following the character of the words, is much more effective and earnest than the bang and clatter, intended to depict the furious sea, in Wagner's *The Flying Dutchman*.

The *Sea-Pictures* should be in every contralto's *repertoire*, for they have the dual possessions of supplying the modern demand for a pleasing tune, and of being a worthy issue from the pen of a master.

OPUS 38. ORATORIO, "THE DREAM OF
GERONTIUS." MEZZO-SOPRANO, TENOR
AND BASS SOLI.

Produced at the Birmingham Triennial Festival of
1900.

The Poem by Cardinal Newman.

This is perhaps the composer's most famous work
and permanently consolidated his claim to world
fame. The main feature that makes this probably
the greatest *oratorio* ever composed, is the tremendous
psychological characterisation of the whole. Elgar
swept away the need for the conventional *arias* and
thumping choruses found in *The Messiah*, *Elijah*
and other *oratorios*, and in their place gave us something that is alive with human interest, gripping every
hearer from start to finish. That is why we believe
that *Gerontius* is the supreme *oratorio*; we have expression, not mere form; living and highly emotional
characters, not stage dummies. *Gerontius* is above
all a monument of art, totally different to anything
that went before it. The *libretto* is captivating to the
human soul, for the question of after-life will always
arouse the interest of man, and Elgar interpreted
it in a remarkably vivid manner. It is significant
too, that the religious Elgar, so often referred to, is
not of primary importance here.

In his later *oratorios*, *The Apostles* and *The Kingdom*,

F

the religious object is painfully obvious, but in *Gerontius* the human element is predominant.   The work
vitally interests ourselves as human beings more than
any religious connections it may have.

The story of the poem commences at the bedside
of the dying Gerontius, who experiences a strange
feeling of abandonment coming over him and calls
on his friends to pray for his soul.   The various Holy
Beings are called upon to save him and the dying
man nerves himself to meet his Creator, reciting the
beliefs of his religion until,

> " I can no more : for now it comes again,
>   That sense of ruin, which is worse than pain,
>   That masterful negation and collapse,
>   Of all that makes man."

A feverish terror now assails him :—

> " Some bodily form of ill
>   Floats on the wind, with many a loathsome curse
>   Tainting the hallowed air, and laughs, and flaps
>   Its hideous wings,
>   And makes me wild with horror and dismay."

He calls on Jesus, Mary and Joseph for help.   The
friends also pray for his rescue, quoting examples from
the Scriptures of the Lord's mercy.

Gerontius now wishes to sleep ; it is, as expected,
the sleep of death.

The Priest and Assistants send the soul on its

journey in the name of a long list of Holy Beings,
concluding the first part of the work.

Part two opens with the soul of Gerontius musing
over its awakening, strangely refreshed :—

" . . . How still it is !
   I hear no more the busy beat of time,
   No, nor my fluttering breath, nor struggling pulse ;
   Nor does one moment differ from the next."

The Soul now feels itself borne gently along, and
hears " heart-subduing " music. The voice of the
Angel is now heard as she looks back on her task of
guiding the " child of earth " through its life.

The Soul ventures to address her, asking the reason
of its not being at the Judgment Throne of God.
" I had ever believed," it says,

" That on the moment when the struggling soul
   Quitted its mortal case, forthwith it fell
   Under the awful Presence of its God,
   There to be judged and sent to its own place.
   What lets me now from going to my Lord ? "

It is assured that they are hurrying " with extremest
speed " to the Judgment Throne. The Soul asks why
no fear of the Presence assails it, since on earth it
lived in terror of the day. The Angel tells it that
the earthly fear is the reason for its not fearing now.
The Soul is speaking of its " Serenest joy " when,

as they near the court, a fierce pandemonium is heard. Affrighted, it enquires the reason. The Angel tells him that the sullen howl :—

" Is from the demons who assemble there,
    Hungry and wild, to claim their property,
    And gather souls for hell . . . "

The evil-spirits rave and scoff at " Low-born clods of brute earth " aspiring to dwell among the saints, and after some gabble about their being the rightful owners of the " realm of light " and their crowns given to " psalm-droners, canting groaners " and other apparent rogues, turn their restless panting,

" Like beasts of prey, who, caged within their bars,
    In a deep hideous purring have their life,
    And an incessant pacing to and fro."

to laughing the saints to scorn :—

" What's a saint ?
        One whose breath
    Doth the air taint
        Before his death ;
    A bundle of bones,
        Which fools adore,
    Ha ! Ha !
        When life is o'er."

Opus 38

The souls also come in for criticism :—

> " Virtue and vice,
> A knave's pretence.
> 'Tis all the same ;
> Ha ! Ha !
> Dread of hell-fire.
> Of the venomous flame,
> A coward's plea.
> Give him his price,
> Saint though he be,
> Ha ! Ha !
> From shrewd good sense
> He'll slave for hire ;
> Ha ! Ha !
> And does but aspire
> To the heaven above
> With sordid aim,
> And not from love.
> Ha ! Ha ! "

The Soul not seeing the demons, enquires whether it shall see the Master. The Angel tells it that for one moment it shall see the Lord, whose glance shall gladden, but also pierce :—

> " Learn that the flame of Everlasting Love
> Doth burn ere it transform . . . "

The voices of the choir of Angelicals are now heard singing *Praise to the Holiest*. As they go on we notice they sing of the Soul's approaching agony, when its stains shall be burnt out. It has no fear, for it says, " My soul is in my hand." This, by the way, must be a feat of considerable agility ; the Soul that now carries itself in its hand was only a short while back being carried in the Angel's palm ! In addition to this it is a puzzle as to whether a soul has a hand ; and whether there is a sort of sub-soul for it to carry ! !

A " grand mysterious harmony " now floods the Soul and the celestial choir are again heard singing praises of God. A feeling of intense excitement pre-vails after this, for the Angel tells that they are now in the veiled presence of the Lord. The Soul hears the voices of his friends on earth, praying at his bedside.

Before the Throne stands the great Angel of the Agony :—

" The same who strengthened Him, what time He
    knelt
Lone in the garden shade, bedewed with blood."

This Angel can best plead for the tormented souls, and now begins a long prayer for the Soul of Gerontius, calling on Jesus by all the things He suffered to show mercy. With all due respect, we cannot help wonder-ing however this Angel gets through the millions upon millions of souls that leave this earth, if it recites this prayer for each. As also a large number

of people die at the same time on this earth, it is
admirable that no traffic confusion appears to occur
as to who goes first, but, of course, the finite mind
cannot conceive the infinite.

A moment of acute suspense occurs as the Soul
goes before its Judge. It returns :—

" Consumed, yet quickened, by the glance of God."

It cries out to be taken away, to dwell, happy in its
pain, in the " lowest deep " till the time comes to
rise and go above to Him in everlasting Peace and
Glory.

The Souls in Purgatory are heard crying out for
deliverance.

The Guardian Angel now once more takes the
Soul, this time dips it in the penal lake and it sinks
down and down until it has at last disappeared :—

" Farewell, but not for ever ! brother dear,
 Be brave and patient on thy bed of sorrow ;
Swiftly shall pass thy night of trial here,
 And I will come and wake thee on the morrow."

The Souls in Purgatory are heard again and are
followed by the Choir of Angelicals singing *Praise
to the Holiest* once more. The work closes with the
usual *Amen*, although Elgar has imparted much
distinction to it, for the tone is long and placid.

There are many parts of the *libretto* which seem
fanatical to us, for instance, we believe in the exist-

ence of " Purgatory " as much as we do Jack's Bean-
stalk or Alice's Wonderland, but the whole is vivid
and imaginative, Elgar's music fitting in exactly
with the words.   In fact if the poem is read and felt,
the music will be found to recapitulate the impression gained thereby.   It would be superfluous and
an intrusion to attempt a detailed analytical account
of the work when such a one as Jaeger's *Analytical
and Descriptive Notes* exists, more especially as this
writer was in direct communication with the composer when writing it, which was originally done for
the first public performance.   The whole account may
be had for a shilling.   It may be worth while, however, glancing at the *Prelude*, which has been in-
corporated with the *Angel's Farewell* as a concert piece.

The *Prelude* recapitulates the leading themes of
the work.   A solemn motive of Judgment (*Lento
mistico*) opens the piece and is followed by a restless
theme, portraying the fear of Gerontius.   This is also
followed by a new motive, expressive of religious
beliefs.   The work now proceeds in a restless, undulating manner, rising to a passionate outburst,
being the appeal for mercy.   This dies away and is
succeeded by an eloquent passage, full of poignant
feeling.   It rises to a great *fortissimo* statement of
Prayer.   This, too, dies away and soon a lovely,
soothing melody is heard, later used as the theme of
the Priest and Assistants sending the Soul on its
journey from earth.   It is repeated twice, the second

time being of great power and very impressive. As
before, the outburst dies away, this time a stroke of
the gong is given and the earlier motives are heard
very subdued. In the concert version, this is now
succeeded by the lovely strains of the Angel's farewell
to the Soul as it disappears in the penal waters.

It is notable that within a year of its first performance at Birmingham, the *oratorio* was performed
in German at Düsseldorf (December, 1901), and repeated at the Niederrheinische Musik Fest in May,
1902. The effect of this was clearly felt in England,
for the public now took a great interest in a work
which they had not hitherto accepted, owing to its
original character. With the famous speech of
Strauss its fame gradually extended until to-day
the annual performance at the Royal Albert Hall,
London, is as important as the festivals of the older
works. The performances now attract an enormous
audience, rivalling that of *The Messiah*.

One of the most magnificent performances ever
recorded occurred at Liverpool on March 15th, 1919.
The composer himself conducted, and under his
direction the work seemed to have an almost magical
effect over the audience, so powerful was the profound
gravity and realism brought out by him.

Buckley tells us the interesting manner in which
the work was composed. Like Beethoven, Elgar
loved Nature for his inspirations, and he would take
his sketch book with him when he went out, jotting

down the ideas whenever they occurred. Slowly the apparently incomprehensible maze of notes assumed a great whole, and at the time of the commission from Birmingham, the composer was almost ready with the work in its present form. He had been studying the *libretto* for ten years !

OPUS 39. SIX MILITARY MARCHES FOR ORCHESTRA, "POMP AND CIRCUMSTANCE."

" *Like a proud music that draws men to die*
Madly upon the spears in martial ecstasy,
A measure that sets heaven in their veins
And iron in their hands,
I hear the Nation march
Beneath her ensign as an eagle's wing ;
O'er shield and sheeted targe
The banners of my faith most gaily swing,
Moving to victory with solemn noise,
With worship and with conquest, and the voice of
  myriads."

(Lord de Tabley).

The above lines were taken by the composer as a motto for his music in this opus number. The circumstance under which the idea of the marches originated was Elgar's feeling that the soldier should not always march to poor stuff. He had mixed a lot with military men and believed that the military

march, a quick step, should be worth marching to.
He therefore conceived the idea of treating it on
symphonic lines, so as to be sure of his music being
suited to the concert room, while at the same time
justifying its title. The marches comprise some of
the most popular music of the day, and are notable
for their brilliant and stirring character.

No. 1. *in D. Allegro Con Molto Fuoco.*

Produced by the Liverpool Orchestral Society, at
Liverpool in 1901.

First Played in London at a Promenade Concert,
Queen's Hall, on 2nd October, 1901.

*Dedicated to My Friend, Alfred E. Rodewald, and the
Members of the Liverpool Orchestral Society.*

This is not only the most popular of the series,
but one of the most widely known pieces of modern
music. It is particularly brilliant in character and
appears to make a distinctly national appeal to
audiences. The bold introduction brings us to the
magnificent, swinging march tune. The theme is
continued with equal brilliance, with an idea that is
transferred to the bass. Repetition, in which the
arresting introduction is prominent, brings us to the
Trio (*Largamente*), afterwards immortalised in the
Coronation Ode as *Land of Hope and Glory*. So
national is this tune in spirit, that it was not infrequent,

during the Great War, for an audience to fervently sing it to the orchestra's accompaniment. The theme is first given out *piano* (*cantabile*) and repeated *Molto Maestoso*, each time in the key of the sub-dominant. It is really an inspiring tune and now has the honour of being one of the finest national songs of England. The first section now returns and, with great splendour, a mighty unison passage ascends to a grandiose rendering of the *Trio*, this time in the tonic key. The march ends with brief allusions to the opening theme.

No. 2. in A Minor.   Allegro Molto.

Produced with No. 1.

First Played in London at the Same Concert as No. 1.

Dedicated to my Friend, Granville Bantock.

Not the least happy part of this march is its dedication to the famous contemporary of Elgar. True genius will recognise the gift in others ; Professor Bantock is a warm admirer of his great countryman, but Elgar equally admired his friend.

The march is rather overshadowed by No. 1, and is smaller and less ambitious. It opens with a spirited theme, after a sharp introduction of two bars, which is worked up to *fortissimo*. The snappy theme is repeated and a broad, typically Elgarian melody enters.

The opening theme is heard again and is followed

Opus 39

by a new idea, which is afterwards varied, given out
in wood-wind and lower strings. Some allusions to
the opening theme bring the march to a conclusion.

No. 3. *in C Minor.   Con Fuoco.*

Coypright 1905.

Dedicated to my Friend, Ivor Atkins.

The *C Minor March* is rather gloomy and foreboding. It opens with a mysterious theme, the
drum-beats on the weaker accents giving an impression of nervous apprehension. A *crescendo* leads
into a more brilliant melody. The opening theme
is repeated with different effects and the *Trio* section
presently enters with a dignified tune, which is
presently succeeded by another theme of equal
dignity.

The first *Trio* theme is recapitulated, and soon the
first two themes of the march are heard again. The
music is then considerably invigorated by fast scale
passages and soon by a powerful *coda*, opening with a
grandiose version of the first *Trio* theme. Fragments
of the two early themes are heard, and then the *Trio*
melody comes out with a brazen accompaniment for
the brass. The jerky idea of bar three of the opening
Trio theme is made much of, and the march ends
with a brilliant recurrence of the close of the first
section. The piece is a bid for something bigger than
the foregoing numbers and is mistakenly neglected.

No. 4. in G. Allegro Marziale.

First Performed on August 24th, 1907, at a Queen's
Hall, London, Promenade Concert.

*Dedicated to my Friend, Dr. G. Robertson Sinclair,
Hereford.*

The fourth march is a return to the broad, healthy
atmosphere of the first. It opens with a stirring,
heroic theme, the beats of the bass-drum and clang
of the cymbals being particularly effective. The
theme is repeated an octave higher, each statement
being concluded with a characteristic little figure for
strings. Some strong passages occur and the work
increases in its martial aspect. The first section is
brought to a disciplined booming close in a short *coda*,
which brings us to the *Trio*, the melody of which is
one of the finest that Elgar has written in this style :—

Nobilmente   *Melodia Marcato*

It is afterwards repeated with fuller scoring. The opening theme returns and concludes with some decisive chords, which make way for a grandiose version of the *Trio*, this time in the tonic key. The *finale coda* is constructed on the opening idea, and ends with great vigour.

It has been suggested, after close examination, that this march is a masterful diversion on, or evolution of, the *March in D* (No. 1). We do not propose to contradict nor support this assertion. The one may be a wonderful construction on the other, or on the other hand it may be only Elgar's same voice on a single subject. We do believe, however, that the fourth march is a distinct advance on its forerunners, being both more inspired and finer in orchestral colour. It is therefore pleasant to be able to relate that the *March in G* almost rivals its companion in D. in the matter of popularity ; in other ways it is decidedly superior, especially in the strain of sentiment that runs through it.

Nos. 5 and 6 Not Published.

OPUS 40. CONCERT-OVERTURE, FOR
ORCHESTRA, " COCKAIGNE " (IN LONDON
TOWN).

First Performed on June 20th, 1901, at a Royal
Philharmonic Society Concert, at Queen's Hall,
London.

*Dedicated to My Many Friends, the Members of
British Orchestras.*

Cockaigne is the most popular of Elgar's three large
overtures. Composed about the same time as the
first two *Pomp and Circumstance* marches, it reflects
in many places, the broad, British, and almost vulgar
spirit of the victorious military events of the period.
The overture opens with a swinging *scherzando* theme,
the little figure of three reiterated semiquavers giving
the impression of gaiety. This theme is succeeded
by a still more sprightly tune, and the two are developed with great exuberance until a passage of some
dignity announces the theme of the nobler Londoner.
This is indicated *Nobilmente*, and is at once lofty and
sustained.

With a return of the cheerful atmosphere, the brass
have some brilliant work, but soon a mood of peace-
fulness comes over the whole, and after a few cheeky
ejaculations, the episode representing the lovers
occurs. This is followed by a new theme, which is
the sole property of the couple, and the music is now

strikingly tranquil and expressive, becoming still more so in the elaboration of the love scenes.

The romantic atmosphere, however, is suddenly squashed by the pert tune of the London street-boy. His theme is happily and significantly derived from that of the nobler Londoner, although the element of fun is naturally irresistible. The music becomes increasingly jerky until presently the opening theme appears *fortissimo*, presently associated with the lovers' theme. The *Nobilmente* now enters softly, followed by the concluding strains of the lovers over *arpeggio* figures, the whole of this portion forming one of the most beautiful in the work.

As this serene atmosphere becomes enjoyable, the jaunty, swinging tune of a military band is heard in the distance. The lovers make several attempts to resume their peaceful conversation, but the growing activity of the urchins and approach of the band makes this impossible at the moment. The music continues to increase in intensity until at last, with a blaring splendour, the band passes by. The passage is strikingly imaginative, the din of drums, bells and triangle, the shrilling of piccolos, and the brazen tune in the brass, combine to make up a most exhilarating and realistic effect.

After the street-boys' glee has been testified, the opening theme appears under a sparkling little accompaniment. This is followed by a thump, thump, thump, that unmistakably tells of another body of musicians. This band is a stationary one, however, as the sounds come no nearer and it turns out to be a Salvation Army meeting. The tune is discordant with the accompaniment, but as soon as one makes an attempt at perfect harmony, the other obligingly shifts into a different key. Peace comes to the lovers again through the medium of a neighbouring church, the music now being engaged with *contrapuntal* working.

The street-boy turns up again, and his theme is mingled with that of the lovers as they leave the church. The opening theme appears vigorously in the trombones, the whole being colourfully treated. The military band approaches again, and passes by with all its former swagger and magnificence. A big *ritardando* passage now occurs and leads to the final statement of the nobler Londoner theme. The utmost splendour is now used, and the broad tune comes out in the full strength of the orchestra, now joined by the organ. The overture concludes with a last, vigorous reference to the opening theme. Altogether the *Cockaigne Overture* is a clever work. In places it is inclined to be rather vulgar, but that is because of Elgar's endeavours to obtain local colour of the Bank-Holiday London. The work is not to be counted among the finest of the composer's symphonic achievements, although it is often played and well known. The expressiveness of passages appertaining to the lovers, and the noble dignity of the *Nobilmente* theme rescue it from the commonplace, which its other themes take it perilously near.

OPUS 41. TWO SONGS.

It appears that Elgar is resting after his particularly fruitful period that we have noticed. There is nothing of exceptional interest about these songs ; they belong to those productions with which Elgar filled up the gaps between his greater works, a proceeding which almost every great composer favoured. Such a period of masterpiece upon masterpiece, *Caractacus*, *Variations*, *Sea-Pictures*, *Gerontius*, *Pomp and Circumstance*, and *Cockaigne*, could not go on for all time.

OPUS 42. INCIDENTAL MUSIC, FUNERAL MARCH AND SONG FOR MEDIUM VOICE, FOR THE PLAY, "GRANIA AND DIARMID," BY MESSRS. GEORGE MOORE AND W. B. YEATS.

Dedicated to My Friend, Henry J. Wood.

The incidental music is short, but contains some refined and delicate orchestration. It opens with some significant horn calls, afterwards joined by the trumpets. Some passages lead up to a melody of compelling wistfulness, leaving its impression on the listener. It passes through various instruments and dies away, concluding the thirty-seven bars of incidental music.

The *Funeral March* opens *maestoso*, which is very impressive in this case. The oppressive heaviness and gloom generally connected with music of this type is absent, although there is a natural air of melancholy about the whole. A new theme enters, but the march continues its solemn course until a drum roll and trembling gong marks the close of this section. The lovely, sad melody of the incidental music enters, now in rather splendid orchestral colouring. After this the first march theme returns and is again followed by the second.

Although some outbursts occur, the *Funeral March* is subdued and bears an air of sad, but generally calm resignation. It is a true expression of the composer's views on death.

In a letter to the author, written early in 1919, Elgar referred to the inevitable as merely a departure from this sphere.

It is not to be expected, therefore, that frantic terror will be found in the *Funeral March*, and on the whole we prefer its character to the moody trudging of the *Dead March in Saul* or the heavy draperies and obscurity of Chopin's *Funeral March*. Beethoven's two examples we admire for their enormous power and absence of sickliness, but we believe that these should only be associated with great men. For a second choice after Elgar, the *Intermezzo Funebre* from Edward German's setting of *Richard III.* is a fine example. It is worth considering that if these examples by Elgar and German were used in place of the sickly odour of Chopin, the power of music would aid us not to regard death as a necessarily horrible occurrence.

The song occurs in Act One of the play. It is written in a pleasing manner and is set to the words of W. B. Yeats, *There are Seven that Pull the Thread.*

OPUS 43. TWO SKETCHES, FOR ORCHESTRA, " DREAM-CHILDREN."

" . . . *And while I stood gazing, both the children gradually grew fainter to my view, receding, and still receding till nothing at last but two mournful features were seen in the uttermost distance, which, without speech, strangely impressed upon me the effects of speech : ' We are not of Alice, nor of thee, nor are we children at all. . . . We are nothing ; less than nothing, and dreams.* We are only what might have been.' " . . . (From *Dream-Children :* a *Reverie*—Charles Lamb.)

These two exquisite little pieces owe their existence to the above quotation from one of Charles Lamb's *Essays of Elia.* Elia is telling the children some tales of their grandmother, when he sees them slowly fade away.

The pieces are of wonderful delicacy and show the master hand in orchestration. An air of wistfulness runs through them both and the only surroundng which can give them their true significance is the fireside.

No. 1. *Andantino* (*espress. ma semplice*). The first piece opens with a quiet expressive theme, in the gently rocking rhythm of 12–8 time. This is followed by much that is contemplative and beautiful, although the whole piece is only twenty-four bars long. It is a miniature of wonderful contents, simplicity always hand in hand with deep feeling.

No. 2. *Allegretto piacevole*. The second piece is longer and commences in a more animated fashion. A lovely allusion to the first number is made by a recalling of its theme, which is then echoed in an expressive manner by the 'cellos. The wistful melody appears in its original form at the end and, at the conclusion, gradually fades away.

OPUS 44. CORONATION ODE, FOR SOLI, CHORUS AND ORCHESTRA.

Composed (by request) for the Grand Opera Syndicate, Covent Garden, London, for the State Performance, June 30th, 1902.

Dedicated (*by Special Permission*) *to His Most Gracious Majesty, King Edward VII.*

Lyrics by Arthur Christopher Benson.

The *Coronation Ode*, despite its being composed for a state performance, comprises some of the most inspiring national music.

1. *Introduction, Soli and Chorus, " Crown the King."* A massive, pompous introduction, in which the various themes of the work are heard, serves to announce the splendour of the occasion and presently ushers in the first chorus, *Crown the King with Life.* The four soloists also have some matter, the net result being very majestic and imposing.

2. *Chorus, " Daughter of Ancient Kings."* This chorus is not quite in Elgar's best vein, but there is an implied spirit which cannot fail to attract attention.

3. *Bass Solo, and Tenor and Bass Chorus, " Britain, Ask of Thyself."* This is a fine, rousing section, brimming over with national spirit. It is all as bluff and hearty as the traditional John Bull.

4. *(a) Soprano and Tenor Soli, " Hark, Upon the Hallowed Air." (b) Quartet (Soprano, Alto, Tenor and Bass) " Only Let the Heart be Pure."* The writing of these is scholarly and contains some typical Elgarian matter, showing the composer in his more serious vein.

5. *Soli and Chorus (unaccompanied), " Peace, Gentle Peace."* This is of a noble quality and full of real and sincere feeling. There is a dignity and beauty that is more a personal reflection of the composer than of any particular function. Mention must be made of the *libretto*, which is of a high quality throughout the Ode, but here surpasses itself in poetical expression.

6. *Finale. Contralto Solo and Tutti, " Land of*

Hope and Glory.'' At Queen Alexandra's request, the *Trio* from the *Pomp and Circumstance March in D,* was used as a setting to the *finale* of the ode.

It here appears in a magnificent form and is always capable of arousing the utmost enthusiasm. We believe that Mr. Newman has made a mistake in subjecting this song to his favourite sport of '' poking fun.'' He has more than once tackled the wrong article, and to say that a song which has won its way entirely because of its inspiring character '' can hardly be called a success,'' is rather too individual an opinion.

There is always a tendency, of course, to criticise anything that gains popularity among the people, owing to the cheap music that generally finds a haven among them, but we believe that a really stirring piece of good music will find an equal, if not superior position, among the masses, who provide the intellectual wealth of the nation. We fail to note any gigantic defects in the song arrangement ; it is healthy and bold in spirit, its tune is musical and its harmonies interesting. The like cannot be said of Beethoven's attempts, in which Mr. Newman has so much faith, although not studying, as he says, the nationality of a composer.

The outcome of it all is that we share in the general acclamation of *Land of Hope and Glory* because it is a fine song and not because Elgar or any other Englishman wrote it. In the same way we fail to appre-

ciate Beethoven's songs, because they are generally
poor. To worship them because they were written
by Beethoven is Jumboism, which a critic should
beware of.

There is hardly a person in England who does not
know *Land of Hope and Glory*, but we neither uphold
nor condemn it on these grounds.

There are millions in England who have never
heard a Beethoven song, but are we to extol them as
classic masterpieces solely for this reason ? Mr.
Newman has said that he is not going to acclaim a
composer because he is English. Neither are we, but
it is determined that he shall have a fair chance. It
is a much easier task to criticise a man who is fighting
his way to fame than one who has acquired it. Remarks on the former will bring forth divided opinions,
but to attack the public idol may be to bring down
highly concentrated wrath.

At the present day this Jumboism has reached such
a pitch, that even the first and second symphonies
of Beethoven are held up as greater masterpieces than
the best of Haydn and Mozart ! We devoutly hope
that Elgar will always remain to be appreciated by
people who really know the deeper side of music and
not merely the weight of a name. To give Mr. Newman his due, we do not believe he is under this craze,
for he has described Wagner's early overture, *Rienzi*,
as vulgar in places, but he has schooled himself deeply
in the established classics and only turns his attacks

on the living school. If only he would see the real
worth of the younger English composers and extol
them in the same manner that he does the older
masters, he would go down to posterity with them.
It is now no feat to see the greatness of Beethoven
and Elgar, therefore they are seldom attacked, except
where justified, but to see and extol the genius of
John Ireland, Frank Bridge, Arnold Bax and others,
requires a certain amount of courage and conviction
in opinions.

OPUS 45. FIVE PART-SONGS, FOR MALE VOICES, UNACCOMPANIED.

Words Translated from the Greek Anthology by
Various Writers.

No. 1. *After Many a Dusty Mile.*
No. 2. *Feasting, I Watch.*
No. 3. *It's Oh, to be a Wild Wind.*
No. 4. *Whether I Find Thee.*
No. 5. *Yea, Cast Me From Heights of the Mountains.*

These are written in a musicianly manner, tinged
with much poetical feeling. Properly rendered they
are fine works, particularly *Whether I Find Thee*, and
the delightful *It's Oh! to be a Wild Wind.*

OPUS 46. MS.

OPUS 47.   INTRODUCTION AND ALLEGRO FOR
STRINGS (QUARTET AND ORCHESTRA).

First Appeared in March, 1905.

*Dedicated to Professor S. S. Sanford, of Yale University,
U.S.A.*

(*Moderato Allegro.*)   This is one of the finest works
ever written for a stringed orchestra.   The immense
volume of tone which the composer obtains from the
instruments is amazing, even in these days of richness
in string-writing.   The work remained in manuscript
for some time and is said to have originated in Wales,
where the composer was attracted by the sound of
distant singing in which the cadence of a falling third
was particularly pleasing to him.   This impression
was later joined by another, that of a song heard in
the Wye Valley.

The music is essentially open air quality, being
strong and animated, with a broad, commanding
beauty in its Welsh theme.   The solo quartet consists
of the usual two violins, viola and violoncello.   The
orchestra is composed of the usual strings, but additional variety is obtained by *divisi* treatment.

The *Introduction* opens with a preliminary theme
and is followed by another, which is used (in the
major key) as the first theme of the *Allegro*.   After
these two have been dealt with, we hear a suggestion
of the Welsh theme.   This is dwelt upon and then

the preliminary idea returns. A pause marks the end of the *Introduction* and the beginning of the *Allegro*.

This commences with the theme already referred to. It has the typical rise and fall of an Elgar melody and is developed at some length. The second subject is given out by the solo quartet and is very simple in character, its *staccato* rendering being particularly effective. After the preliminary theme of the *Introduction* has been heard again, the second subject is worked towards a stately half-close.

The next idea to catch our attention is a fugal one, still in the same healthy and vigorous mood of the whole. After this has been dealt with, the three foregoing themes of importance are heard again, followed presently by the Welsh theme, which comes out in the full strength of the strings. It is especially fine in its open and direct character, and presents, of course, the greater aspect of the work. The *Allegro* ends with sundry references to its first theme.

We feel that no one but Elgar could have written such a gorgeous work for the strings. It is not the fanciful Boccherini or the graceful Mozart, or even the lyrical Grieg that is at work, but a veritable giant of tonality; a magical creator of rich and sonorous beauty.

Sir Henry J. Wood's performance is a triumph of British art and British players; we do not know of any other conductor who obtains such magnificent results from this particular work. Presumably it is because of his intricate knowledge of string interpretive powers.

OPUS 48. SONGS. No. 1, " PLEADING," WITH ORCHESTRAL ACCOMPANIMENT.

Words by Arthur L. Salmon.

Dedicated to Lady Maud Warrender.

Pleading stands out as one of Elgar's most beautiful songs. His conception of the words is of the utmost sincerity. The expression is very pure and noble, and the song needs a singer of refinement fully to portray its beauty. Here again we feel called upon to mention an artist ; one who has done much, by his noble interpretation, to make the song appear in its greatest form. This is the English singer, John Coates, who has sung the song when the composer himself was an ordinary member of the audience.

Pleading remained a long time in manuscript before its publication.

OPUS 49.   AN ORATORIO, "THE APOSTLES."
First Produced at the Birmingham Musical Festival,
October, 1903.

Composed in Longdon Marsh, 1902-3.   Words Selected
from the Holy Scriptures.

*Composer's Note.—The ancient Hebrew melody
(Ps. xcii.) commencing on page 21 (Vocal Score) is
quoted by kind permission of the publishers, Messrs.
Augener and Co., from the volume edited by Ernst
Pauer, whose broad and appropriate harmony is retained in a few bars. Use is made of a portion of the
Gregorian tone (freely adapted)—" Constitues eos "—
the Gradual in which power is promised to the Apostles
and their successors for all time. This theme, and other
details concerning the music, will be found in the analysis.*

E.E.

Concerning this *oratorio*, Elgar said, " It has long
been my wish to compose an *oratorio* which should
embody the Calling of the Apostles, their Teaching,
and their Mission, culminating in the establishment
of the Church among the Gentiles." The idea of
such a work originated when the composer was a
school boy.

Like *Gerontius*, *The Apostles* soon found favour
among the German critics, who, to their credit, always
judge a living composer on his merits. The work

was produced in German at the Niederrheinische
Musik Fest, Cologne, in 1904.

The *oratorio* is a step forward from its predecessor,
but will hardly ever rival it in popularity. The
human interest is not so earnestly aroused, although
the work is deeper and perhaps more intellectual.
It is profoundly religious in sentiment, but at times
it is only the very meaning of the text that is the
dominant point. Elgar apparently conceived the
work entirely by its religious aspect which had such
meaning to him, that he sometimes forgets the purely
musical aspect. Because a certain passage in the
Scriptures contains something that is significant to
him, it appears that this fact should make an instant
appeal to the listener by its own significance, the
music merely being the means of presentation.

To certain sectarians the *oratorio* would be a great
work for the very fact of its religious aims. To the
person who looks for something intensely gripping,
like *Gerontius* ; something that appeals to human
nature and not to any particular sect, the result is
not exactly as expected. We do not of course imply
that the music is of inferior quality, indeed, it is of a
genuine high order. The greatest parts are those
of Jesus and Judas, the latter being regarded in the
modern manner, *i.e.*, as one who wished to betray
Jesus only in the hope that He would perform such
a miracle, that the world would acknowledge Him.
With these two characters Elgar leaves his *Apostles*

scheme and writes in a human and more vivid emotional style ; it is the man that comes uppermost and not the creed.

The whole work itself is connected with the choosing of the Twelve Apostles, and various Scriptural characters up to the time of the Crucifixion. The Ascension and the doings of the disciples afterwards, are brought in at the end of the work, but the main idea of this period is continued in the next *oratorio*, *The Kingdom*, (Op. 51).

The analysis of *The Apostles*, by A. J. Jaeger, is indispensable to those who would look into more fully the beauties of this great work, which will always be regarded as the erection of the great master. On better acquaintance it becomes less laboured than before, and we are continually reminded of the power and energy with which the whole was conceived. Only an exceptional genius and architect could have made it.

We would regard it as merely fighting for length to give an analysis or idea of the story when the former has already been referred to as the work of Elgar's own official, and the latter has been done by the Rev. Canon Gorton (*Interpretation of " The Apostles "*), a friend of the composer. We certainly dealt with the story of *Gerontius*, but this is a work upon which much interest is extended, and as such could not be passed over without supplying what we hope was a requirement.

OPUS 50. CONCERT OVERTURE, FOR OR-
CHESTRA, " IN THE SOUTH " (ALASSIO).*

First Produced at the Elgar Festival, Covent Garden,
London, 1904.

Dedicated to my Friend, Leo F. Schuster.

This huge overture is very important in Elgar's
career as a symphonic master, being the last trial
flight, as it were, before the first symphony. On the
technical side we notice the broad scope of modern
tonality, the freedom of modulation and development
and the super-brilliance of the orchestration. On
the æsthetical side we see the wonderful pictorial
phrases, the last opportunity, as it happened, for
Elgar to be described as a programmist, the glowing
warmth of expression and all the brilliant features of
the composer brought forth in the impassioned light
of Southern romanticism.

The following lines were chosen by Elgar as a
motto for the *Overture* :—

" . . . What hours were thine and mine,
In lands of palm and southern pine,
In lands of palm, of orange blossom,
Of olive, aloe, and maize and vine."
(TENNYSON, *The Daisy*).

* Alassio, North Italy,

H

"... a land
Which *was* the mightiest in its old command
And *is* the loveliest ...
Wherein were cast ...
                    ... the men of Rome!
Thou art the garden of the world."
                    (BYRON, *Childe Harold*).

The opening theme (*Vivace*) commences without preamble and is at once glowing and vigorous. After, it is continued with a counter-subject above, an air of serenity comes over the whole, until at the fifty-fourth bar a magnificent full version of the opening theme is given out. This is followed by a pompous passage leading to a *Nobilmente*, which, although a finer outburst, is inferior in expressive power to examples in other Elgar works. The *In the South Overture* is not exactly a grand and noble work, although a tuneful and highly colourful one. The inclusion of a *Nobilmente* passage in it appears to be the result of a habit, for the surrounding atmosphere is not of the type that can set off the typical Elgarian indication. It is significant that a later statement of the same passage is more appropriately indicated *Grandiose*.

The theme grows in intensity until at last a reaction sets in, culminating in a theme of tender simplicity. This gentle lullaby continues until a change of key, time, speed and expression brings the second subject,

full of restless and romantic spirit. The theme has a
soothing continuation, after which we arrive at the
working out section.

This commences with some references to the tender
theme, but the dominant atmosphere, however,
seems to be passionate until a sense of hardness comes
over the whole. This increases until some iron-like
strides lead to a passage of enormous strength.

Elgar gives two more lines from the Tennyson poem
to describe this :—

"What Roman strength Turbia showed
In ruin, by the mountain road."

He further tells us that he has " endeavoured to
paint the relentless and domineering onward force
of the ancient day, and to give a sound-picture of
strife and wars, the drums and tramplings of a later
time." This is an unfortunate statement for the
champion of pure music to have made, but, as we
have said, it was the last occasion of a " programme "
work. After some consideration of the powerful
theme, a restless figure is heard, continually growing
in excitement and culminating in some wild, frenzied
outbursts. The Roman theme, however, a little
subdued, introduces order again, concluding with a
show of its former strength. On its disappearance
the wildness breaks out again, but a calmer spirit
at last settles over the whole.

Four bars marked *ppp, molto tranquillo,* serve to usher in a gently rocking theme.

This was the thought by many, at first, to be an *Italian canto popolare,* and is still known as such, but the composer assured us that it was entirely original. It is curious that anything of a distinctly peculiar trait, relative to the country of its inspiration, is set down as an allowable and agreeable form of plagiarism. It will be remembered that Sibelius had some difficulty in establishing the *entire* originality of his well known national piece, *Finlandia.*

The development of the " Italian " melody is very beautiful, particularly loving is the effect when the opening theme is heard as an inner part. The tender theme is also afterwards worked in, and at last the *Canto popolare* dies away unfinished.

The recapitulation commences *pianissimo* with the opening theme, soon working up, however, to a *fortissimo.* The earlier themes appear in all their glowing colours and *Nobilmente* afterwards enters *ppp,* working up to a full statement of the second half of the tender theme. The opening idea now appears in an altered form, mostly suggestive ; the tones of the Glockenspiel are heard and at last an animated passage brings us to the great *finale.* The *Nobilmente* is now marked *Grandiose* and is given out with gorgeous colour and tonality, brilliantly augmented in the lower parts by the opening theme. This vast array of splendour increases in intensity, culminating in a last, thunderous statement of the opening theme.

The *In the South Overture*, inspired by the Italian winter during the composer's visit of 1903-1904, particularly in the splendid beauty of the Vale of Andora, surpassed in tone colour anything that Elgar had then written. The only point where it is not equal to his other large works is in spiritual intensity. The overture has actually been described as the finest of Elgar's three large examples, but this impression may easily have been made by the ponderous length of the work and its super-brilliance of colour.

It is not to be supposed that *In the South* would have benefited by the inclusion of any great emotional spirit, for it is purely an expression of admiration for the beauty of Italian scenery, tinged throughout with romantic, but not deeply expressive, warmth. The whole work is a spontaneous outburst rather than a pre-conceived masterpiece.

OPUS 51. AN ORATORIO, " THE KINGDOM."

First Produced at the Birmingham Musical Festival, October, 1906.

Composed Plas Gwyn, 1905-6. Words selected from the Holy Scriptures.

Dedicated to A.M.D.G.

The Kingdom is a continuation of *The Apostles*, demonstrating how taken the composer was with writing something that " should embody the Calling of the Apostles."

The present work is essentially a religious one and linked with *The Apostles* by several themes of this work that are used. As a whole it contains some of the purest and most beautiful music of the serious Elgar, but again we are conscious of the importance with which the composer regards the actual circumstances of the various scenes. His very life was poured into the two last *oratorios* and it is with bitter thoughts that we look on the studied neglect of them, and yet we are only too conscious of the reason. To the devout person of a certain sect they are great works, unfortunately not necessarily because of the music, but owing to the deep significance of the events. To the ordinary music-lover, much of the music is uninteresting, his attention is upon art, when it should be upon the story, conscious only of the sympathy of the music.

The handful of musicians, like Ernest Newman and others, who really see the the enormous power of the composer in the construction of the last two *oratorios*, are not enough to influence choral societies to perform them. We do not see any hope of them becoming standard *oratorios* like *Gerontius*, for the majority of people could not fasten sufficient interest in the religious aspect ; not having been trained to a certain significance of the characters, the music would often become boring to them. *Gerontius* serves one master, human nature, and is a phenomenal success. *The Apostles* and *The Kingdom* are after the religious and the musical, with the result that trying to serve two masters generally has ; they have become dispensible to both. We do not in the least agree with the neglect of the two, for their beautiful and masterly architecture would always be accorded admiration. In point of structure they are greater than *Gerontius* and greater, indeed, than many works of many ages.

Again attention must be called to the writings of A. J. Jaeger. His *Analytical and Descriptive Notes* on *The Kingdom* are as convincing as those on the other two *oratorios*. A greater realisation of the true scope of the work is given, more than we could ever hope to give here. By it, with the score of the work at our side, we are convinced that *The Kingdom*, like its companions, is as spiritually different to the *oratorios* of Handel and Mendelssohn as the great music dramas of Wagner are to the operas of France and Italy.

OPUS 52. "A CHRISTMAS GREETING," FOR TWO SOPRANOS, WITH ACCOMPANIMENT FOR TWO VIOLINS AND PIANOFORTE, OR FOR ORCHESTRA, SOLI AND CHORUS.

Words by C. Alice Elgar.

This is conceived in a charming and friendly manner, the words being especially warm hearted. The composer again appears to be resting after his strenuous efforts in the immediately preceding works.

OPUS 53. FOUR PART-SONGS.

No. 1. *There is Sweet Music*, (8 Parts).
No. 2. *Deep In My Soul*, (6 Parts).
No. 3. *O Wild West Wind*, (8 Parts).
No. 4. *Owls* (An Epitaph), (5 Parts).

These are worthy examples of the English School's greatness in this branch of music. The songs possess musicianly qualities of the highest order, while the feeling is always serious and beautiful. The expectation aroused by each title is generally realised, and altogether the part-songs are little bits of genius, giving ample opportunity of expression and skill to the singers.

OPUS 54. PART-SONG, " REVEILLE," (T.T.B.B.).

This song is not marked as Op. 54, but on enquiring of the composer for the name of this number, we received the information here set down. The part-song is very interesting and extremely suitable for male voices because of its literary aspect. It can be sung with stirring effect if the right spirit is caught.

OPUS 55. SYMPHONY No. 1, IN A FLAT.

Composed 1907-1908.

First Produced by Hans Richter, at a Hallé Concert, Manchester, on December 3rd, 1908.

First played in London on December 7th, 1908, by Richter and the London Symphony Orchestra.

Dedicated to Hans Richter, Mus. Doc., True Artist and True Friend.

No. 1. *Andante (Nobilmente e Semplice). Allegro (Appassionata).*

No. 2. *Allegro Molto,* leading into

No. 3. *Adagio (Cantabile).*

No. 4. *Lento-Allegro.*

The intention to compose a symphony had revolved in Elgar's mind for many years, although it was at Richter's and Jaeger's suggestion that he finally composed one for publication. Although the present work is known as the first symphony, among the composer's early MS. are, or were, several other attempts, but it is doubtful whether they are anything more than experimental in value.

The *A Flat Symphony* may be regarded as Elgar's supreme achievement in symphonic form. At the time of its composition he was at the zenith of his powers, although it proved to be only the first of his greatest orchestral works. In the symphony we find the sublimest expression of his spiritual outlook and there is perhaps no other work, excepting the *C Minor Symphony* of Beethoven, which affords us so vivid and complete an insight to the psychological aspect of a great man. Although Elgar's work has been described as " spiritual program music," the composer himself assured us that it has no programme, being nothing more than " a composer's outlook on life."

On this basis the whole symphony may be viewed as a musical expression of the conflicting emotions of the ideal and the reality. It is a work that will probably never become popular in the ordinary sense of the word, for it is far too vast and problematical. Its themes are not easily remembered, excepting perhaps the great leading or central theme, and its length is almost inordinate. This latter fact is the great drawback to both of Elgar's symphonies. It may convey a sense of vastness to construct such spun-out works, but in this respect we much prefer the ability shown by Beethoven in expressing his thoughts in a concise, but none the less acceptable and masterly manner.

Elgar's symphonies are too mentally indigestible for the average concert goer, and it is not really possible to appreciate them unless the hearer is acquainted with the composer's idiosyncrasies as expressed in the earlier works. Elgar's symphonies are not in demand by the general public, in spite of what our fellow enthusiasts may say ; they are only appreciated at their true worth by those who are his admirers, and happily their number is now very imposing.

Whatever the extent of public appreciation, however, there can be no disputing that Elgar's two symphonies are the most monumental creations of their kind since Beethoven's day ; their slow movements alone are equal in expressive power to any music that we are familiar with.

The great power of the *A flat Symphony* lies in its unity of purpose. Throughout its many moods, which range from bitter and almost violent intensity to serene simplicity, there appears to be but one object, which is typified by the great theme that opens and closes the work. Although the *Symphony* has the usual four movements, the extensive transference of themes from one to another makes these divisions little more than formal breathing space.

Thanks to Richter's undying enthusiasm for Elgar's work, the *Symphony* met with enormous success and publicity at first, and was played about a hundred times within a year of its production ! Afterwards, however, it was allowed to lie on the shelf and it is only due to Landon Ronald and one or two others that it was not allowed to be forgotten. Under Mr. Ronald's hand the work appears as an immortal masterpiece, but unfortunately there is at present no conductor who has the experience and insight to extend public appreciation of it, although, of course, there are several fine readings of the work, most notable being those of Sir Henry J. Wood and Mr. Appleby Mathews, the Birmingham exponent of Elgar.

Perhaps the most wonderful part of Mr. Ronald's work is the attention and applause he obtained for both symphonies at Albert Hall Sunday afternoon concerts.

1. The symphony is constructed on the classical plan with modern freedom and extension, including the transferring of themes from one movement to another. It has also a relationship with the *Cyclic* plan of Franck.

The scoring is for the modern orchestra, without the addition of any unusual percussion instruments, but including, of course, bass-drum and cymbals.

The slow introduction commences with two bars in which the lower strings and timpani give out the key note. The noble and dignified melody that follows must be impressed on the memory, for upon it the whole work is dependent. It is, and will be referred to as, the *Leading-theme*. It appears in many places throughout the work and always brings a benign influence to bear on the psychological aspect. More than once does it wrestle with the darker elements, eventually triumphing by reason of its sustained and lofty character. The theme is repeated softly and afterwards in fuller scoring, in which its greatness and power become evident. Its actual length is twenty-one bars, but if we quote half-a-dozen it will give a general idea of its character :—

The *Allegro* (D minor) provides a sharp and opposing contrast to the introduction and would appear to be symbolic of the whirl and stress of actual life. The harps have some effective and prominent passages leading to a change of time to 6–4, which soon brings a more tranquil melody. After a time we may define the beautiful second subject (F major) commencing high in the violins. It floats along with the utmost serenity and during this mood some particularly Elgarian passages are heard.

With a return of the opposing theme all is commotion again and the music proceeds with much ferocity, significant perhaps of the force of the darker elements. The leading theme, however, soon appears and sheds its benign influence over the whole. A reminiscence of the opening *Allegro* is noticed and there are traces also of one of the lesser themes.

The development section commences with a sustained and penetrating statement of the leading theme, which is followed by colourful versions of various others. After a time an extremely foreboding and new motive enters which, with the appearance of contrasting powers, serves to illustrate still more the bitter and relentless force of the opposition. The second subject appears in a strengthened aspect and adds to the power of the emotional contrasts. A long drum roll on F sharp continues the awesome impressions and brings a further sense of foreboding and mystery over the whole.

The appearance again of the leading theme is very welcome, but it is soon followed by the opposing theme, which ushers in the recapitulation section. The atmosphere carries on the idea of antagonism, but in time the leading theme once more intervenes. The darker forces are not easily disposed of, however, and they are worked up to an outburst of enormous strength, comprising one of the most striking and bitter passages in the work.

The *Coda* commences softly with the leading theme prominent. The foreboding idea appears, but is soon obscured by the gentle, yet commanding influence of the greater force, which guides the movement to a wonderfully calm and peaceful ending.

2. This movement (F sharp minor, 1–2 time) may be regarded as a big *Scherzo* and its whole character is impetuous and fiery. It opens with four introductory bars, a feature of which is the commanding force of a

figure of three notes for the bass drum, expressing the dominant mood of the whole.

The swiftly moving theme appears immediately after this introductory figure and is accompanied by a significant figure alternating the leading note and tonic. The theme is rounded off each time by a little idea in quavers. It is repeated an octave higher and succeeded by a joyous figure which, after a *glissando* for harps, is also repeated.

A new theme now enters in the dominant minor and has a swinging march-like air, although its character is slightly foreboding. It is repeated by the full orchestra after which the joyous figure is heard again and also a new idea is noticed. A fiery version of the opening theme, however, soon claims foremost attention, but it eventually dies away and the music modulates to B flat major. In this key we find a lovely, serene melody floating over a droning accompaniment. It is ultimately followed by an equally lovely clarinet theme and the two unite in forming the middle section of the movement.

The opening subject now reappears in the original key, the second melody of the middle section being heard above. In the ensuing discussion we notice the prominence of the joyous figure.

The march theme is soon heard *fortissimo* and is presently accompanied by the opening subject, given out by the lower strings and wood wind. The two great ideas now proceed along in a powerful union, their positions being presently reversed, showing their equality of importance, the march theme being heard in the lower strings and wood wind (double bassoon and bass-clarinet being added), trombones and tuba. The two middle themes are heard again, but as the whole proceeds, we are conscious of a seriousness coming over it. There is no longer the impetuous animation and the new spirit becomes very pronounced when the opening subject appears augmented to quaver triplets. Presently it appears still more restrained, being now in crochets. The figure of the leading note and tonic becomes especially significant and finally all is expressed in mournful and mysterious chords, the long drawn out and persistent F sharp being particularly gloomy in effect. A deep *pizzicato* becomes more and more infrequent until nothing is left except the mournful F sharp.

The last part of this movement is particularly imaginative and enigmatic. In the last few bars it is as if the whole trembled on the brink of extinction, but without a break the *Adagio* enters :—

3. The opening melody is that of the impetuous first theme of the preceding movement, but now so transformed in spirit and augmented in time value as to have an almost new character, which is absorbed in tender, yet sad meditation. A noble climax gives out the ever strengthening essence of the leading theme, this time combined with *scherzo* subject in its more familiar form, but not, of course, exuberant.

Opus 55

An original little descending phrase follows and the
music continues its peaceful course until an expressive
chord is reached.

After this point the drum gives out some impressive
beats and the beautiful second subject is heard. This
has a counter subject which clearly suggests the
influence of the leading theme. The ensuing elaboration that follows is full of colourful gems in orchestral
effects and can only be appreciated by the ear. The
first melody is heard again, and after a time a new idea
appears, the most beautiful, perhaps, in the whole
work. Its appeal is direct and simple, and goes
straight to the soul of the listener. From this point
the music becomes more and more retiring until at
last, with a final expression of purely Elgarian touch,
it fades completely away.

4. The *finale* opens with a painful and sudden
realisation of the reality. A faint and mysterious
tremolo from the strings (last desk only) and bass drum
ushers in the foreboding theme from the first movement. Against this, however, is soon heard a suggestion of the leading theme and the contrasting forces
give out some impression of intensity. The greatest
force assumes supremity and an arresting final chord
ends the *Lento* and prepares for the glad tune of the
Allegro. After this the benign influence is felt again
and soon the second subject, in the form of a *cantabile
melody*, exercises control. This is succeeded by a
springing march, which imparts life and activity to

the whole once more. It grows higher and higher until the whole orchestra takes it up at full strength.

After the outburst has died away the leading theme is heard with great dignity, although still quiet. After many exquisite and colourful passages the opening *Allegro* returns with all its gladness. It is followed by the march which strides on to a mighty climax, after which a sweeping downward *glissando* for the harps makes way for the great leading theme, *Grandioso (poco largamente).*

The whole now proceeds with indescribable magnificence and nobleness. The colour grows richer and richer, and the triumphant ideal is vividly evident as the second subject is heard. The end comes with one last and mighty allusion to the great theme, given out by the brass, and in this exultant spirit ends Elgar's outlook on life.

OPUS 56. PART-SONGS.

No. 1, ANGELUS (TUSCANY).

This is a creditable and tuneful specimen, possessing distinction and originality.

OPUS 57. PART-SONG, " GO, SONG OF MINE."

This is a very fine work and enjoys much favour among provincial choral societies. It is in six parts and throughout is woven together with thorough musicianship. The expressive qualities are of high grade and altogether the song is very worthy of the attention bestowed upon it.

OPUS 58.   ELEGY, FOR STRINGS.
ADAGIO.

Although very short, this is an exceedingly beautiful work and reveals the composer's power of expression in its most simple aspect. The whole mood of this little gem is lofty and sustained, never leaving its quietude, yet from start to finish confiding and impressive. The string writing is, of course, very sonorous and confirms the fancy that we have seen a glimpse of the greater Elgar.

OPUS 59. A CYCLE OF SIX SONGS, WITH ORCHESTRAL ACCOMPANIMENT.

The numbers published at present are *Oh, Soft Was the Song* (No. 3) ; *Was It Some Golden Star ?* (No. 5) ; *Twilight* (No. 6). They comprise some of Elgar's loveliest songs and are to be commended to all who wish for something more enobling than the ordinary ballad song. It is impossible to describe here the many exquisite touches of vocal and instrumental wriitng, but the arrangement with pianoforte accompaniment will bring them within reach of any who wish to hear them.

OPUS 60. FOLK-SONGS (EASTERN EUROPE) FOR TENOR OR SOPRANO, WITH ORCHESTRAL ACCOMPANIMENT.
No. 1. " THE TORCH." No. 2. " THE RIVER."

These numbers are most remarkable for their intensity and realism. The words and their source of inspiration afforded a fine chance for powerful emotional writing, and Elgar did not fail to grasp it. Although the atmospheric sense has a lot to do with the fine effect of these two songs, there is no doubting the work of the master hand that enables them to be so strikingly presented.

OPUS 61. CONCERTO IN B. MINOR, FOR VIOLIN AND ORCHESTRA. No. 1. ALLEGRO. No. 2. ANDANTE. No. 3. ALLEGRO MOLTO.

First Produced, November 10th, 1910, at a Concert of the Royal Philharmonic Society at Queen's Hall, London.

Soloist : Fritz Kreisler. Conduced by the Composer.

Dedicated to Fritz Kreisler.

Although the *Violin Concerto* has been described as a pendant to the first symphony, it has little in common with the psychology of the earlier work. It presents no direct conflict of emotions or spiritual problems, neither does it pursue obviously, any great ideal.

Apart from this question of relationship, however, the *concerto* stands independently as one of Elgar's most representative works. Almost every page of it is remarkable in some way or other for its lovely inspirations, and throughout we come upon passage after passage of sheer beauty and expressive power.

It was to be expected that Elgar, with his knowledge of the violin's capabilities and encouraged by the success of the first symphony, would write a fine *concerto* and the production, especially as Kreisler was to be the soloist, was looked forward to with some eagerness. The promised work did not fail to come up to the expectation of the enthusiasts and was soon taken up by the solo violinists of the day. The effect of time only served to enhance its artistic value and within ten years it had passed naturally into the ranks of standard *concertos*.

The main features of the work are its wealth of expression, both for solo instrument and orchestra, and its richness in harmonic and instrumental colour. As regards the purly technical elements, a heavy claim is made on the soloist, but only as a means to obtain the æsthetical effects mentioned ; there is not one bar in which opportunity for mechanical ability stands alone. The orchestra is naturally of equal importance with the solo instrument.

The whole constructive aspect of the *concerto*, however, is best summarised by Margaret Fairless, one of its finest interpreters, who says, " The *concerto* is to me as one great song or poem, or as the sea, full of restless, passionate emotion rising to great climaxes and yet at all times mysterious. It is a great work and one of the noblest. Like most other great works it is not a solo, but rather a symphony for orchestra and violin ; a huge *ensemble* work. I do not think that there is any other work for the violin which gives the artist a freer chance of individual rendering."

To those who believe in significance as opposed to coincidence, the fact that the opus number of Elgar's *Violin Concerto* is the same as that of Beethoven may be interesting. Its key is the relative minor of that of the older work, but this is more a technical point concerning the tonality of the solo instrument.

I. The *Concerto* is reasonably scored for the usual wood-wind, brass, timpani and strings, with double-bassoon and tuba *ad lib*. It is based on the classical plan with modern freedom, including the transference of thematic material from one movement to another, the omission of a *cadenza* in the first movement and the inclusion of an accompanied one in the *finale*.

The *Allegro* opens with an orchestral *tutti*, in which the several themes are stated and developed at some

length. The first subject consists of four distinct
motives which, being heard in succession and linked
together, almost satisfy the formal demand for a
single theme. Each motive, however, has its own
particular sphere of activity. The last is pondered
over for some time before the second subject appears.
This latter takes the form of a lovely and tender
melody and is heard as dialogue between wood-wind
and strings. It will be better quoted later on at its
fuller exposition.

With the exception of the third, the orchestra
now dwells on the opening motives and on the *finale
cadence* the solo violin makes its appearance—*Molto
largamente* (*nobilmente*). There is no rhetorical display calling attention to the soloist, but only utter
seriousness reflecting the deeper aspect of the whole.

After a while the impassioned quietude gives way
to greater animation, but never for a moment descending to mere technical display. The motives of
the first subject are developed with much variety of
colour, the fine treatment of the brass being especially
pleasing. After this we come to the fuller exposition
of the lovely second subject. It is echoed by the
orchestra and altogether twenty-one odd bars serve
to show how lovingly the composer regarded this
theme.

After the development comes the usual recapitulation, in which the attention of the listener is never
allowed to relax, so fine is the material to be heard

again and so subtle and many are the harmonic and orchestral colours. The movement ends with a vigorous reference to the dignified No. 1 motive.

2. The *Andante* (*B flat Major*) is one of the most idyllic movements Elgar ever set down, being from start to finish a poem of tenderest, although at times fervent, expression. It is founded on a song-like theme of simple character given out by the orchestra. This floats calmly along until the key changes to C major, when a new figure, of impressive quietude, enters. The middle section is ultimately reached and is responsible for a further theme, given out by the solo violin, and the music becomes now more strenuous with that peculiarly passionate intensity of the composer. The *Nobilmente* motive that follows in the orchestra should be noted, as it plays an important part in the final movement. Both are of course heard again in the recapitulation of this movement, which is more especially notable for the charming passages allotted to the solo violin. As the end draws near the whole atmosphere becomes wrapt in peaceful contemplation, which grows more and more refined until at last the music seems to die away in ineffable serenity.

3. The *Finale* brings back the everyday surroundings with *vivace* and *fortissimo* in the foreground. A second subject is given out by the solo instrument (*cantabile e vibrato*), and in due course the *Dual-Rondo* form brings the recapitulation. In this, the

first subject is treated with much variety of harmony, the solo violin playing an important part.

The music grows in liveliness until the presence of the *Nobilmente* from the *Andante* is felt. This ultimately leads to the *Cadenza*, which contains some of the most elevating passages in the work. The orchestra, with strings mostly divisi, now gives out a quiet and profound version of the No. 1 motive from the first movement; the solo violin, with equal gravity, answers with No. 4. A mysterious effect is obtained by the *pizzicato-tremolando* given to the first half of the strings. The players are directed to drum softly on the strings with the fleshy part of their fingers, the effect obtained being like the distant murmuring of Æolian harps. It floats round the soft strains of the solo and the whole atmosphere soon becomes peculiarly ethereal in character.

After a time the music increases in significance till an unaccompanied passage for the soloist finishes on a trill, under which is heard the *Nobilmente*, now very soft and sustained. This is followed by the orchestra further giving out an agitated version of the No. 1 motive, but the solo instrument almost immediately takes the interpretation and the orchestra is hushed. In a mood of profound and lofty sentiment the *cadenza* comes to an end. Margaret Fairless, who should know best, has said of it, " that unlike others, far from being a means of personal display for the soloist, it is more of a soliloquy or a dreamy, intimate review of the work."

The return of the vigorous mood brings back again the worldly impressions, but the influence of the deeper elements are still felt and soon the *Nobilmente* appears again. The second subject is recalled and is followed by the first, which is treated with great dignity. Attention is drawn by the full and impressive chords of the solo violin until a *Coda*, seven bars long, brings this most beautiful of Elgar's works to an end.

The *Concerto* has achieved world-wide popularity, but it is fortunate that the interpretations of two historic combinations have been recorded for the gramophone. These two are Albert Sammons and the Queen's Hall Orchestra under Sir Henry J. Wood, and Marie Hall and the Symphony Orchestra under Sir Edward Elgar himself.

A work which offers so many opportunities for the soloist to prove his, or her, emotional powers is naturally one that calls for a discussion of various renderings. The famous Kreisler, who first performed the work, seems to have fully realised its underlying feeling, almost overshadowed as it sometimes is by the wealth of colour.

Albert Sammons and Marie Hall have also given refined and impressive renderings, and Zacharewitsch must be mentioned for his enthusiasm, which even carried the work to Italy.

One of the most serious, although at present not
too widely known, interpretations is that of Margaret
Fairless, whose opinions we have already quoted in
connection with the *concerto*.   In the rendering of this
artist we find the full realisation of the finest qualities
of the work, showing us the very soul of Elgar.   It
is not a mere professional performance, but a sincere
and inspired insight ; altogether one which may be
taken as very near the most faithful and authoritative
that we shall hear at the present day.   The attitude
of the player herself towards the *concerto* may be
quoted, again using her own words, " I love the
concerto and hope to play it very many times in the
course of my musical career.   Each time I play it
something new appears.   I always feel too small to
do it justice ; it needs a great genius."   This is an
admirable form of mind and we can recommend its
modesty to other players.   We also quite agree that
the work needs a " great genius " to interpret it, but
at present we do not know of any individual, however
great he or she may be in other works, who so spon-
taneously reflects the true spirit of Elgar as Margaret
Fairless herself.   There may be criticisms of her playing in other great *concertos*, but this does not interest
us here, as our business is only to show where Elgar's
concerto may be heard under the most favourable
circumstances, as far as the soloist is concerned.

OPUS 62. ROMANCE, FOR BASSOON AND ORCHESTRA.

The fact that Elgar, in his youth, was a performer on the bassoon makes this work rather interesting. It is written in a pleasing and effective manner, affording the instrument many fine opportunities for displaying its not inconsiderable artistic worth. It is seldom, if ever, performed, although the reason for this is beyond ordinary comprehension.

OPUS 63. SYMPHONY No. 2. IN E FLAT.

First Produced, May 24th, 1911, at the Third Concert of the London Musical Festival (1911), by the Composer and the Queen's Hall Orchestra.

Dedicated to the Memory of His Late Majesty King Edward VII.

This Symphony, designed early in 1910 to be a loyal tribute, bears its present dedication with the gracious approval of His Majesty the King.—March 16th, 1911.

" *Rarely, rarely comest thou,*
    Spirit of Delight." (Shelley).

No. 1. *Allegro Vivace e Nobilmente.*

No. 2. *Larghetto.*

No. 3. *Rondo-Presto.*

No. 4. *Moderato e Maestoso.*

Encouraged by the great success of the *first symphony* and *violin concerto*, Elgar was not long in returning to the great domain of symphonic writing. It is interesting to note how eagerly the great composers pursued the great art-form when once they had tasted its greater possibilities. Beethoven was thirty before his first symphony appeared, but within three years the *D Major* was ready. Schumann neglected the composing of his beautiful *B flat Symphony* until he was thirty-one, but the second was produced in the same year. Brahms had reached his forty-fourth year when the *C Minor* was ready, but the great *D Major* followed it within a twelvemonth. Returning to our own composer, we find that, true to the national characteristic, he was more behind than any of his great predecessors, being fifty-one at the time of the *A flat Symphony's* production. Within two years came the *Violin Concerto* and six months after this the present symphony. They were all written at the height of his creative power, however, and are monumental achievements, worthy to stand beside the greatest symphonic works extant.

The second symphony is a complete psychological contrast to the first. In place of contrasting emotions and their struggles, we have a gorgeous wealth of almost unbounded joy. The work pulsates with life and beauty almost without interruption; even the lofty slow movement reflects the dominant mood, although with pronounced thoughtfulness. The poem of Shelley from which the composer took the symphony's motto is of rather melancholy a character, but the music is more an expression of the rare spirit itself than the regret of one to whom it is lost, as told in the poem. Like Beethoven again, Elgar was past the summer of his life before he realised a musical expression of joyous ideal. Far too many composers occupy their finest years with creations expressive of despairing problems, the unknown and similar gloomy outlooks, and it is not until the years of retrospection come that they are apparently aware of the joy of life.

The most striking feature of the symphony is its gorgeous wealth of colour, which even exceeds that of the *violin concerto*. At times it becomes so mysterious and filmy, that the thematic material almost disappears from sight. Like its predecessor, the work met with a great reception at first and was repeated within a week, but it has unfortunately been more shamefully neglected than any other great work of Elgar, excepting, perhaps, *Falstaff* and *Polonia*. In 1920 it met with a brilliant revival and was played twice in London within a month, in addition to Landon Ronald's tour with the Scottish orchestra in the North, where the symphony was the success of the season.

1. The symphony is scored for modern orchestra without anything more striking in the percussion than a side-drum. The movement opens right away with a bounding theme in 12–8 time and is split up into smaller motives in the same mood. The third bar

of the opening idea should be noted as it often appears, always symbolic of the joyous spirit :—

After the rich opening has created its impressions, a new melody appears in the same joyous mood. Altogether, in fact, we may quote three new motives before the appearance of the real second subject. The three are as follows :—

Needless to say the orchestration is exceedingly full
and rich, reaching its zenith in a furious, but not less
joyful outburst.   This dies away in a typical synco-
pated passage leading to a lovely and expressive new
melody :—

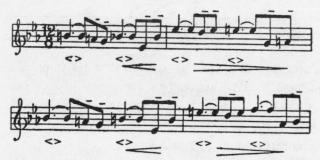

After some treatment of this the real second subject
enters, in the form of a penetrating theme for the
celli :—

The lovely melody is now further developed, followed
by earlier matter.   These are worked up to a big

climax in which the second subject figures prominently, although not in its original form.

The working out section consists of sundry modifications of the first subject group, but is more remarkable for its striking episodical matter. A complete change seems to come over the surrounding atmosphere, everything becoming mysterious and subdued. An enigmatic idea floats through the whole, the colour of which is unearthly and weird. The whole passage, with its piercing discords and far away throbbing of the drum, calls upon the most fantastic trend of the imagination.

After a time some of the opening material returns in a restrained form, but in the final section, however, the former vivacity returns. The scoring is still very rich and, tempered by a quiet expressiveness, the whole works up to free and intense joyousness. Near the end the symbol of happiness is given out *fff* and repeated with a great swell of exhilaration. The movement concludes with a brilliant and varied rendering of the tonic chord.

2. The *Larghetto*, which has been described as one of the grandest slow movements since Beethoven's day, commences with soft and mystic chords, followed by a dignified and thoughtful theme :—

Its central section is broad and glowing. After a time, a new passage appears, having a peculiarly wistful melody :—

(It will have been noted by this time, that a feature of the symphony's thematic material is the number of themes that run in thirds). This theme merges into a further one and from now onwards the whole grows in indescribable richness, culminating in a magnificent *Nobilmente*.

This is the end of the procession of themes and repetitions now commence. These are all done with elaborate tints and the end comes with a last reference to the first theme and the soft chords of the opening.

3. This movement is remarkable for its super-brilliant orchestral effects. Its main theme is typical of the *Scherzo*-like whole, which is however called a *Rondo* :—

After this another appears :—

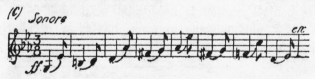

As the movement proceeds, we are conscious of the many little ideas that spring up in various places until after a time, a deeper and decidedly strange force begins to be felt. In the midst of the general gaiety it is very puzzling, particularly when the almost shapeless accents of the timpani, bass and side drums begin to grow in intensity.

The whole culminates in a tremendous flow of sound, after which the original mood returns and the movement ends in a brilliant and direct fashion.

4. The principal theme is direct and characteristic of all Elgar's *finale* movements :—

It is treated generously until the arrival of a second and equally typical theme :—

Its second part, which is not quite so pronounced in

rhythm, is made much of. After this a broad and
march-like melody appears, more typical than ever
of Elgar's last movements :—

After this the two first ideas are treated with many
varieties, until at last a climax is reached in the form
of ascending sequences of the third theme. A passage
maked *piu tranquillo* brings back the symbol of
happiness, now augmented, but still singularly expressive of freedom and joy.

As the music proceeds it grows more and more
subdued, but always in complete serenity until at last,
seven bars from the end, there comes a quick *crescendo*.
This immediately dies away again ; the tonic chord
is given out *fortissimo* and held for two bars ; then,
without another effort, it dies completely away, leaving
us in a mood of profound, but happy contentment.

The close of the *E flat Symphony* is quite as effective
in its way as the great outburst of the A flat, and
altogether the work is one that is a striking and indispensable contrast to its great predecessor.

OPUS 64. OFFERTORIUM, " O HEARKEN THOU."

Composed for the Coronation of King George V.

There is nothing vitally important about this work although the level of the writing is good. The vocal score, English or Latin words, may be purchased for twopence.

OPUS 65. CORONATION MARCH (1911), FOR ORCHESTRA.

This is another work that owes its existence to the crowning of the king in whose reign Elgar received the Order of Merit. It is written in the composer's large march style and was of interest to those who wondered how the greater writing would effect this type of Elgar's genius. There is a notable increase in the general magnificence, the piece appears, indeed, as if a giant were handling the form. At the 53rd bar a typical broad *Nobilmente* enters and the conclusion, commencing *Maestoso*, works up to a brilliant and imposing *Grandioso*.

The march is, of course, the surface Elgar, but is extremely appropriate.

OPUS 66. IMPERIAL MASQUE, IN TWO
TABLEAUX, "THE CROWN OF INDIA."

Produced at the London Coliseum, on March 11th,
1912.

Orchestral Suite. First London Performance, September 17th, 1912, at a Queen's Hall Promenade
Concert.

Written by Henry Hamilton.

This was written on the occasion of the visit of King
George V. to his Indian Empire. The artistic worth
of the masque is not monumental, the numbers at
present obtainable being :—

VOCAL SCORE
SONG, " THE RULE OF ENGLAND "
SONG, " HAIL, IMMEMORIAL IND ! "
DANCE OF NAUTCH GIRLS
INTERLUDE
  DO. FOR VIOLIN OR 'CELLO AND PIANO
WARRIORS' DANCE
MARCH, " THE CROWN OF INDIA "
MARCH OF THE MOGUL EMPERORS
BOOK OF THE MASQUE

Of these *The Crown of India March* is interesting,
but the general conception is not an inspired one. It
is fortunate that the work was only written for a
passing occasion.

OPUS 67. CHORAL SETTING OF THE 48TH
PSALM, " GREAT IS THE LORD," FOR ORGAN,
BASS SOLO AND CHORUS.

First Produced on July 16th, 1912, at Westminster
Abbey, London.   Special Service in connection with
the 250th Anniversary of the Royal Society.

This work is described as an " *Anthem for the Foundation or Commemoration of a Church, or for General
Use.*" The composer constructed his own version
of the psalm from both the Authorised and the Revised
Prayer Book. In comparison with the ordinary
anthem the work is somewhat musical in conception,
expression going before formality. The organ and
vocal parts are not extraordinarily difficult, and a well-
trained choir may sing the anthem with fine effect.
There are two great climaxes, while the conclusion is
massive and extremely effective. We would commend the work to choirmasters who have not the opportunity of performing Elgar's larger choral creations.

OPUS 68. SYMPHONIC STUDY FOR ORCHES-
TRA, IN C MINOR, WITH TWO INTERLUDES IN
A MINOR, " FALSTAFF." (" King Henry IV."
and " King Henry V."—*Shakespeare.*)

First Produced at the Leeds Musical Festival, on
October 2nd, 1913, under the composer's direction.

Falstaff is one of Elgar's finest works and deserves
far greater recognition than it receives at present.

The composer here strikes away from his inevitable dwelling on beautiful moments and we have the brilliant wit and humour, kingly dignity and tragedy, found in the life of Sir John Falstaff.

After the *Study's* production at Leeds it was introduced to London by Landon Ronald and the New Symphony Orchestra on November 3rd, 1913. Since then the work has been so carefully ignored that the first performance by the Royal Philharmonic Society on December 5th, 1918 (Conductor, Landon Ronald) was reputed to be only the fourth of its career, a fact that reminds us of the slowness with which Beethoven's works made their way at first.

Throughout, the work abounds with interest not only as regards sentiment, but in the matter of technical ingenuity. Elgar himself supplied the analysis in the *Musical Times* of September, 1913, and we cannot, of course, substitute anything for the composer's own writings, therefore by courtesy of the popular musical journal we reproduce the original analysis, omitting, owing to lack of space, the musical illustrations :—

" FALSTAFF."

By Edward Elgar.

For the Leeds Festival, in October, a *Symphonic Study for Orchestra, in C minor, with Two Interludes in A minor* (Op. 68), has been completed by the writer of these notes. If we take the word " study " in its literary use and meaning, the composer's intention will be sufficiently indicated.

As the work is based solely on the Falstaff of the historical plays (1 and 2 *Henry IV.* and *Henry V.*), in examining it or listening to it, the caricature of *The Merry Wives of Windsor*, which, unluckily, is better known to English playgoers than the real *Falstaff*, must be forgotten. Professor Dowden, after allowing the probable authenticity of the tradition that *The Merry Wives* was written at the request of Elizabeth, says : " Shakspere dressed up a fat rogue, brought forward for the occasion from the back premises of the poet's imagination, in Falstaff's clothes . . . he made it impossible for the most laborious 19th century critic to patch on *The Merry Wives* to *Henry IV.*,"* and it is noteworthy that Morgann, in his essay on Falstaff, ignores the Merry Wives entirely. The real " Sir John Falstaff is a conception hardly less complex, hardly less wonderful than that of Hamlet."† This complexity has been summed up by Morgann as follows : " He is a character made up by Shakespeare wholly of incongruities ; a man at once young and old, enterprizing and fat, a dupe and a wit, harmless and wicked, weak in principle but resolute by constitution, cowardly in appearance and brave in reality ; a knave without malice, a lyar without deceit ; and a knight, a gentleman and a

---

* Dowden.   *Shakspere—His Mind and Art.*
† Dowden.

soldier, without either dignity, decency, or honour."*

The idea that Falstaff is merely a farcical character is entertained so generally that it is necessary to insist on the last clause of Morgann's statement— a knight, a gentleman, and a soldier. He " is by no means a purely comic character. Were he no more than this, the stern words of Henry to his old companion would be unendurable."† " He had been page to the Duke of Norfolk, a fact which certifies to his respectability of position and inferentially to his possessing the instincts of a gentleman ; had associated with John of Gaunt, who certainly would have had nothing to do with a poltroon ; had served for many years in the army and earned knighthood, then a purely military. title . . . takes his soldiers into the thick of the fight where they are soundly peppered, and he himself must have been in great danger, earns from the Prince who supposed him to be dead, a tribute of regret he would hardly have bestowed on one whose cowardice he despised."‡

To this catalogue of honour may be added that Falstaff appears at the Council held in the King's Camp (1 *Henry IV.*, Act v., Scene 1), the others present being the King, the Prince, Lord John of Lancaster, and the Earl of Westmoreland.

It is in " an apartment of the Prince's " that Fal-

Essay on the Dramatic Character of Sir J. Falstaff (1777).   Maurice Morgann.
† Dowden
‡ Deighton.   *Introduction—Henry IV.* : Macmillan.

staff first appears, and the feeling of pleasantry which runs through the dialogue is almost courtly ; Prince Henry apostrophises him as " Thou latter spring ! All-hallown summer ! " Then follow scenes so finely graduated that they exhibit one of the highest flights of Shakespeare's genius—we are shown the inevitable degradation down to the squalid end.

" In the First Part (*Henry IV*.) he takes a whole-hearted delight in himself, in his jollifications, his drolleries, his exploits on the highway and his almost purposeless mendacity . . . In the Second Part his wit becomes coarser, his conduct more indefensible, his cynicism less genial."* He appears many times in the Second Part, but only on one occasion in the Prince's company ; we note almost with pain, the gradual fall from the close companionship to lower and still lower levels until we arrive at the repudiation by the new King followed by the death scene, the peculiarly poignant account of which is given in *Henry V*. " The king has killed his heart," says the Hostess—" The king hath run bad humours on the knight," says Nym—" His heart is fracted and cor-roborate," says magniloquent Pistol, and in the next Act comes the incomparable passage, " A' made a finer end and went away an it had been any christom child . . . for after I saw him fumble with the sheets and play with flowers and smile upon his fingers' ends, I knew there was but one way ; for his nose

* Brandes. *Introduction—Henry IV*. : Heinemann.

was as sharp as a pen, and a' babbled of green fields."*

Hazlitt sums up his study of Falstaff thus : " The true spirit of humanity, the thorough knowledge of the stuff we are made of, the practical wisdom with the seeming fooleries, have no parallel anywhere else . . . In one point of view they are laughable in the extreme, in another they are equally affecting—if it is affecting to show what a little thing is human life."

The musical interpretation, or, as it is preferably called, *Study of the Character of Falstaff*, is practically in one movement, with two interludes, to be noted later, and falls naturally into four principal divisions which run on without break. These divisions are not shown in the score, but it is convenient to cite them as follows :—

I.   Falstaff and Prince Henry.

II. Eastcheap, Gadshill, The Boar's Head, Revelry and Sleep.

III. Falstaff's March, The Return Through Gloucestershire, The New King, The Hurried Ride to London.

IV. King Henry V.'s Progress, The Repudiation of Falstaff, and His Death.

Some lines quoted from the plays are occasionally placed under the themes to indicate the feeling to be conveyed by the music ; but it is not intended that the

---

*I have adopted Theobald's suggestion, now beyond cavil if not beyond criticism.

meaning of the music, often varied and intensified, shall be narrowed to a corollary of these quotations only, and this simple presentation of the composer's ideas makes no attempt to describe the manifold combinations of the themes, the contrapuntal devices and other complexities of the score.

I.

" An Apartment of the Prince's," at Court. " Enter Sir John Falstaff " : we see him " in a green old age, mellow, frank, gay, easy, corpulent, loose, unprincipled, and luxurious."*

This, the chief *Falstaff* theme, appears in varied *tempi* throughout the work, and knits together the whole musical fabric.

The gargantuan, wide-compassed *fortissimo*, first given to the strings in three octaves, exhibits his boastfulness and colossal mendacity :—

" I am a rogue if I were not at half sword with a dozen of them two hours together."

As the scene is mainly a conversation the music consists of a presentation and variation of these themes ending with an impetuous rush—the persuasive Falstaff has triumphed, the dominating Sir John is in the ascendant.

*Morgann.

II.

We are in Eastcheap and plunge into a quicker *tempo* commencing with a theme made up of short, brisk phrases, all of which, used largely in the construction, should chatter, blaze, glitter and coruscate ; no particular incident is depicted, but the whole passage was suggested by the following paragraph :

" From the coldness, the caution, the convention of his father's court, Prince Henry escapes to the teeming vitality of the London streets and the Tavern where Falstaff is monarch. There, among ostlers and carriers, and drawers, and merchants, and pilgrims, and loud robustious women, he at least has freedom and frolic."*

The musical illustration of the Tavern would not be complete without the Hostess and Doll Tearsheet, if not the " dozen or fourteen honest gentlewomen," so a suggestion of the theme associated with this most virtuous company flits across the fabric to find its full expression later.

We now come to more substantial material. Here with his cheery companions is the Falstaff who sings *When Arthur First in Court*, who shouts delightedly at the prospect of battle, *Rare Words ! Brave World !* and who describes himself as " a goodly, portly man, of a cheerful look, a pleasing eye,

*Dowden.

and a most noble carriage," and who "did good service at Shrewsbury."

We now enter on a new phase, the midnight exploit at Gadshill. Want of space prevents the exhibition of the material employed. A strenuous passage depicts the short struggle for the twice-stolen booty, "got with much ease."

An extended *fugato* in quavers, hurried and scrambling, suggests the discomfiture of the thieves, who, after some attempts to repair their disorder, arrive once more in tolerable case at the Boar's Head.

The "honest gentlewomen's" theme, now complete and raised to due importance, runs its *scherzo-like* course until the *Falstaff* theme is interjected, somewhat unsteadily but encouragingly, evolving a *trio* section of uproarious vitality; after the reprise, the knight again attempts speech, but is somewhat more incoherent, vague, and somnolent. Through the heavy atmosphere a strange, nightmare variant of the women's theme floats, and Falstaff sinks down to the heavy sleep suggested by:

"Fast asleep behind the arras; how hard he fetches breath."

The sleep theme is embroidered with much orchestral detail for muted strings, etc., and leads into the first interlude :—

"He was page to the Duke of Norfolk,"

This, a dream-picture, is scored for a small orchestra; simple in form and somewhat antiquated in mood, it suggests in its strong contrast to the immediately preceding riot, " what might have been."

III.

But the man who " broke Skogan's head " does not long dream of the courtly period of his youth. The music, now *fortissimo*, shows a sudden awakening ; a *fanfare* is heard (muted brass), once distant and a second time less remote. All is bustle and preparation for the route, " a dozen captains . . . knocking at the taverns and asking everyone for Sir John Falstaff."

Out of the hurry and confusion Falstaff emerges " to take soldiers up in counties as he goes." The march follows :—

" I have foundered nine score and odd posts."

It is hoped its attendant theme may be a fitting accompaniment to the martial gait of the scarecrow army of Wart, Mouldy and the " forcible Feeble."

On the edge of the battle, the light-hearted knight, who had once before led his men where they were " soundly peppered," jokes in the face of danger with John of Lancaster.

When the army is " discharged all and gone," he decides " I'll through Gloucestershire : there will I visit Master Robert Shallow, Esquire." The march, as we approach the fields and apple-trees, assumes a song-like character, until we rest in Shallow's orchard. Here we have a second interlude, scored as is the first for small orchestra, and again with an old English flavour and as simple in form.

After some sadly-merry pipe and tabor music a passage for muted violas and 'celli occurs.

This mild, bucolic entertainment is suddenly interrupted by Pistol announcing, " Thy tender lambkin now is King—Harry the Fifth's the man." A large and agitated presentation shows Falstaff glorying in the news : " Master Shallow, my *Lord Shallow*, be what thou wilt, I am fortune's steward." The march theme is resumed rapidly, " I know the young King is sick for me "—" we'll ride all night."

IV.

Near Westminster Abbey the new King is to pass with his train ; Falstaff and all his company await his coming among the shouting populace :—

" There roar'd the sea, and trumpet-clangor sounds."

The music takes the form of a triumphal march, founded on the King's military theme with several additional sections. Into them the Falstaff themes are expectantly thrown ; the King's approach is suggested by recalling the merry times of Gadshill, but now the orchestration is heavier and the import serious.

The climax comes, fully harmonized and extended, when the King appears "glittering in golden coat . . . and gorgeous as the sun at midsummer"; then with a rush of quavers, the Falstaff theme is given *fortissimo*, and the King halts. A brief parley ensues, but Falstaff is inexorably swept aside by the King's brazen motto, and the last pitiful attempt at cajolery is rudely blasted by the furious *fanfare* :—

"How ill white hairs become a fool and jester—
I banish thee on pain of death."

Immediately the royal march is resumed, and dies away; the King has looked on his ancient friend for the last time.

In short phrases the decay of the merry-hearted one is shown. The broken man weakens until, with a weird, final attempt at humour we enter upon the death scene :—"He is so shaked that it is most lamentable to behold." The incomparable description has been quoted already; the music is founded on the orchard theme. With many changes of harmony, faltering and uncertain, it goes to the end as if "he played with flowers and babbled of green fields." True as ever to human life, Shakespeare makes him cry out even at this moment not only of God, but of sack, and of women; so the terrible nightmare version of the women's theme darkens (or lightens, who shall say ?) the last dim moments. Softly, as intelligence fades, we hear the complete theme of the gracious

Prince Hal, and then the nerveless final struggle
and collapse ; the brass holds *pianissimo* a full chord
of C major, and Falstaff is dead.

In the distance we heard the veiled sound of a
military drum ; the King's stern theme is curtly
thrown across the picture, the shrill drum roll again
asserts itself momentarily, and with one *pizzicato*
chord the work ends ; the man of stern reality has
triumphed.

In the time of their close friendship the Prince,
thinking him dead, says, " Poor Jack, farewell, I
could have spared a better man," and sadly we say so
now. The Prince, arrived at his kingly dignity,
fulfilled the prophecy of Warwick, " he will cast off
his followers, and their memory shall a pattern or
a measure live."

Their memory does live, and the marvellous
" pattern and measure " Sir John Falstaff with his
companions might well have said, as we may well
say now, " We play fools with the time, and the
spirits of the wise sit in the clouds and mock us."

OPUS 69. ODE, FOR CONTRALTO SOLO, CHORUS AND ORCHESTRA, " THE MUSIC MAKERS."

First produced, October 1st, 1912, at Birmingham.

Conducted by the Composer ; Vocalist, Miss Muriel Foster.

The Poem by Arthur O'Shaughnessy.

It will be noticed that this work was performed before the preceding one, although it is of later opus number. A striking feature of the Ode is the number of themes the composer has borrowed from his other works, in order to give the required musical expression at the right moment. We hear quotations from the *Variations, Sea-Pictures, Gerontius,* the *Symphonies,* the *Concerto,* in addition to phrases of such national airs as *La Marseillaise* and *Rule, Britannia.* Each one of these themes is used here by Elgar because at the time of " making " they expressed a definite mood ; the national phrases also have a certain significance in the composer's mind. We may therefore have a key to the meanings of some of the themes in foregoing works.

It must be borne in mind however, that the majority of the music was new, the quotations being merely episodes. The idea of O'Shaugnessy's lines is fascinating. The music-makers and dreamers, although " wandering by lone sea-breakers " and forsaken of the world, are really, in their art, the makers of history . . " the movers and shakers of the world for ever, it seems." Their dreams are of the morrow, the present time being only the working out of the seeings of past dreamers, and they dwell aloof from their fellow men. The whole spirit of the poem portrays the endless planning of the future by the music-makers and dreamers which is to be the toil and strife of the multitudes.

Elgar fully perceived the significance of the ode to his own calling. He realised how great are the responsibilities of the creative artist in his efforts to renew the art world. The work of to-day is the life-existence of to-morrow. The composer himself speaking of this work said : " The creative artist suffers in creating or in contemplating the unending influence of his creation. Even the highest ecstacy of ' making ' is mixed with the consciousness of the sombre dignity of the eternity of the artist's responsibility."

Elgar was also, however, fully alive to the progressive spirit of the poet's lines and he regarded it as his duty to see that the never ceasing change was one of progress. His final words on the piece depict this spirit.

The work commences with an orchestral prelude marked *Moderato e Nobilmente*. The first theme is passionately agitated, but is soon followed by a second melody, smooth and tranquil. It is typical of Elgar to provide contrast in this way, but the effect is always a welcome one. Soon we notice the sad, contemplative theme of the *Variations* coming out as an inner part in the violas and celli. This is developed and presently the chorus enter with the opening lines of the poem : " We are the music-makers," etc. In the accompaniment are presently heard the solemn opening strains of the *Gerontius Prelude*.

While the dreamers wander by the sea, the familiar air from one of the *Sea-Pictures* is used, but as they realise the far-reaching effects of their work, the music works up to a gripping and thunderous effect. The sadder atmosphere returns, but as the piece proceeds, the reflections of the future bring a great energy, some of the lines having very striking music, including the triumphant strains of the English and French national airs already referred to. A mysterious atmosphere now settles over the music until a passage of great emotional power is made to signify a tribute to the composer's old friend, A. J. Jaeger : " But on one man's soul it hath broken," etc. During this a quotation from the *E flat Symphony* is heard and afterwards the haunting second subject of the *violin concerto*. The noble leading theme of the first symphony is also heard. The contralto soloist has a lovely and always expressively thoughtful part, and from now to the end of the work the mood is mostly one of sadness ; the wistful air of one who too fully recognised the significance of " a singer who sings no more." The Ode dies away with an almost inaudible chord, deeply impressing the mournful spirit upon the listener.

The *Music-Makers* is unlike anything Elgar had before written, the gripping curiosity of the poem being remarkably more vividly realised through the medium of the music. Each individual will have his or her own thoughts on the work, but the human interest in destiny unseen will effect an indescribable similarity of impression, on which rests the never failing interest of O'Shaughnessy's and Elgar's " making." Both men peered into the future and both have created something for it.

OPUS 70. " SOSPIRI," FOR STRINGED ORCHESTRA.

First Performed August 15th, 1914, at a Queen's Hall (London) Promenade Concert.

Dedicated to My Friend, W. H. Reed.

(*Adagio.*) This is a very short work, but possesses a magnificent and penetrating solemnity. It is in reality a miniature slow movement of a symphony, so deep and sustained is its message. It is written mostly in full chords and altogether its attitude is strikingly massive. The dedication is to the famous composer and violinist, the leader of the London Symphony Orchestra.

OPUS 71. PART-SONGS. No. 1. " THE SHOWER." No. 2. " THE FOUNTAIN."

During the intervals between his larger works it will have been noticed that Elgar generally brought out some songs, more often part-songs. These are by no means, however, trifles, in fact they show considerable musicianship and not a little depth of feeling. The English composer can, of course, always rely on a ready market for good part-songs, owing to the wonderful wealth of good choral singing that goes on in the Midlands, Wales and the North. In this respect London does not represent a fraction of musical England, although some of the capital's amateur choirs are excellent. The choral societies of England perform a greater proportion of native works than foreign and the English ballad concert is often a hundred per cent. British. The inference to be drawn from these facts is that Elgar was only supplying a national want when he turned at intervals to vocal music on the smaller scale. The two part-songs comprising Op. 71 are excellent specimens of their kind and easily give the impression of their titles. The interest is always kept alive because the flow of parts seems natural and exclusive to the particular occasion. The second number, it may be noted, is in five parts.

OPUS 72. PART-SONG, " DEATH ON THE HILLS."

In this piece there is considerable power and it presents a fine opportunity for a choir with dramatic spirit. The writing is in seven parts and the title gives the key to the arresting power of the emotions of words and music.

OPUS 73. PART-SONGS. No. 1. " LOVE'S TEMPEST." No. 2. " SERENADE."

These two present a contrast. The first abounds with a free and romantic spirit and is in five parts. The second is in a happy mood and refreshing after the preceding number. The choir that sings these two in succession will have an acceptable opportunity of displaying their command of contrasting emotions.

OPUS 74. CHORAL SETTING OF THE 29TH PSALM, " GIVE UNTO THE LORD," WITH ACCOMPANIMENT FOR ORGAN AND ORCHESTRA.

This piece is in the style of the general anthem with the customary freedom that Elgar gives to expression. There is much that is pleasing and we

remain convinced that Elgar had still retained his
ability to throw religion into a lofty musical interpretation. We do not think it wise to have demanded
an orchestral accompaniment here, although doubtless
it is very necessary to express the composer's ideas.
The larger choral societies with orchestras, however,
are not likely to consider it important enough for
performance, while the smaller concerns would not
gather an orchestra together for the same reason.

OPUS 75. CARILLON, " CHANTONS, BELGES,
CHANTONS ! " (" SING, BELGIANS, SING ! ").

First Produced at the Queen's Hall, London, on
December 7th, 1914.

The Poem by Emile Cammaerts. (English Version
by Madam Tita Brand Cammaerts).

This is the first of Elgar's immortal works directly
inspired by the European War, 1914–1919. It is not
the greatest of them, for it was written in the early
days before the ghastliness of the world calamity had
fully dawned upon England or America. The work
therefore strikes a fiery and martial note, although
contrasted, it is true, by deeper elements. It is far
superior to Elgar's other martial works, for throughout
the piece there is a noble and heroic element ; Belgium's fate at least had been realised by the composer.

In parts it is fired by the indomitable spirit of the great little nation and in others there are somewhat sad reflections of the sadder side of war.

The fame of *Carillon* soon spread all over England and eventually to America, where it was received with tremendous acclamation. Elgar wished it to be used in order to help the Belgian relief work, and it is said that it earned large sums of money for this cause. Early in 1919, during the Armistice period, the piece was produced in Belgium itself and the effect on the audiences was reputed to be memorable. Practical proofs of success were the heavy orders received by the publishers in London for Belgian towns.

The work is ingeniously founded on a ground bass comprised of the descending upper tetrachord of the scale. The main themes are generally striking, for both in the martial and the deeper motives there exists a commanding sense of the source of inspiration. In short the music is as powerful as the words and the whole possesses a scholarly claim in addition to its significance of a certain period. The work may be bought for a couple of shillings as a pianoforte solo version, with English and French words *ad lib*. It is also effective in its organ arrangement.

When the actual war spirit and interest had fallen off, the publishers decided to arrange the whole as an orchestral concert piece and as such it should stand as a work of art.

OPUS 76. SYMPHONIC PRELUDE FOR
ORCHESTRA, " POLONIA."

First Produced by the London Symphony Orchestra
at the Queen's Hall, London, on July 6th, 1915, under
the Composer's direction.

Concert in Aid of the Polish Relief Fund.

Dedicated to Ignatz Jan Paderevski.

Polonia is one of the noblest and most brilliantly
beautiful pieces that issued from Elgar's pen. The
work was written expressly to help the Polish victims,
who afterwards appeared as aggressive reactionaries,
of German " culture," and contains all the best music
of a national spirit as seen by a foreigner. Its orchestration is of surpassing richness, while the general
material is weaved together in a manner that only an
exceptional master could devise. The causes that led
up to its composition are told by the composer himself : " It was suggested two months ago (this would
probably be early in 1915), by Mr. Mlynarski, that a
Polish piece should be written to help Polish funds,
as he told me so much had been done for Belgian
charitable undertakings by the *Carillon*. But the idea
of writing an orchestral fantasy on Polish themes was
not new to me, and curiously enough the suggestion,
or rather the influence, came from Herefordshire.
The heir of the ancient family of Bodenham married,

in 1850, a noble Polish lady, and from their descend-
ant, Count Lubienski-Bodenham—the Squire of
Bodenham while I lived in the adjoining parish—I
heard much of Polish history, thought and feeling
that supplemented mere . book knowledge. Very
deeply regretted, this lovable gentleman died a few
years ago. That some sort of a *Symphonic Prelude*
might be a practical, and perhaps a useful tribute to
my friend Paderewski, for the concert in aid of his
countrymen was the final inducement to weave into
a concise orchestral movement some typical Polish
themes."

From the first it was a subject that Elgar could make
much of, for in the national music of Poland there is
a great amount of human expression.

It will be noticed, in Elgar's statement, how his
principle of giving a work to the world and there
leaving it was carried out even with *Carillon*. He
was told how it earned money for charities and we
may depend on this being information to him, for he
would refrain from reading, in public journals, any
accounts of his works.

The great pianist, but afterwards politician,
Paderevski, to whom *Polonia* was dedicated, received
the work with genuine admiration. Some time afterwards, when he became the first Prime Minister of the
" Independent Polish Republic," the following extract
of a letter received by Elgar from the Polish leader
appeared in the London Press :—

Opus 76

" I heard your noble composition, my beloved *Polonia*, on two different occasions ; deeply touched by the graciousness of your friendly thought, and profoundly moved by the exquisite beauty of your work, I write you a letter of sincere and affectionate appreciation."

The work commences with a few sentences which lead to an original theme of the composer, said to be the motive of his admiration for the Polish people. It is stated *fortissimo* by the brass and is distinguished by its magnificent bearing. The first Polish theme will be noticed by its pathetic and undulating character. The second is heard in the bassoons at first ; it is of considerable length and afterwards is brilliantly stated by the full orchestra. The next theme is the heroic national air of Poland, " *Yesreze Polska nie Zginela !* " (*Poland is Not Lost Yet !*). Soon the Elgar theme is heard and some episodical matter leads up to a quotation from the *G Minor Nocturne* of Chopin. This is given out by the muted strings, accompanied by *arpeggios* in the harps and a far away drum roll, constituting one of the loveliest and most impressive passages in the work. It is afterwards followed by the bold, national opening theme of Paderevski's *Polish Fantasia* for Pianoforte and Orchestra. After this the themes are combined and worked up with great spirit, which reaches its summit on the appearance of the second Polish air, now given out with stirring effect. The wonderful harmonic and orchestral colouring that follows is of too great complexity for literary definition. It is one of music's aspects which defy description, although appreciated by the ear. The *Prelude* fittingly concludes with a magnificent, stirring version of the Polish National Air for full orchestra and organ, the final chords being overwhelming in their impassioned spirit.

After going through *Polonia*, it is not to be wondered at that the composer received a tremendous ovation after its first performance. It will always remain an inspired work of art, a gorgeous treat for those who desire richness combined with musical spirit and scholarliness of the highest order.

OPUS 77. RECITATION WITH ORCHESTRA, " UNE VOIX DANS LE DESERT " (" A VOICE IN THE DESERT ").

First Produced on January 29th, 1916, by Sir Thomas Beecham, Bart., at the Shaftesbury Theatre, London.
(Operatic Season.)

This piece was performed nightly for a week after its production. It was afterwards heard at concerts and introduced to the United States. Sir Edward Elgar himself gave us the Opus number of this, as in print it is not so marked at present. The main idea is an orchestral accompaniment during the recitation of the poem, after the style of *Carillon*. The recitation is interrupted in one part while a song, *When the Spring Comes Round*, is sung by a soprano. The work met with considerable success at first and is well written and interesting. An arrangement for voice and pianoforte is available.

OPUS 78. FANTASY, "THE STARLIGHT EXPRESS."

Produced at the Kingsway Theatre, London, for the first time at Christmas, 1916.

Lyrics by Algernon Blackwood.

The simple and fairy-like charm that runs through the music of this play makes it one of the most delightful things written by Elgar. It is all a refreshing insight to the lovable character of Elgar, standing out like a bowl of fragrance from its great companions on either side. We, who have listened to the great ideas of the symphonies and concertos, the profoundness of the oratorios and other works, experience an indescribable delight on hearing these strains from the fresh green of nature and the innocent joys of fairyland. The greater works show us Elgar the deep thinker and idealist, *The Starlight Express* is the Elgar of real life, the delightful and kindly man for whom there was always affection. Here we do not look up to the symphonic master, but feel with him as one among us and enjoy his music accordingly.

M

The only published form of the play now catalogued is the arrangement of three songs with pianoforte accompaniment and the pianoforte suite. The latter is of importance and it is with it that we shall enjoy the music. It is, however, magnificent to relate that the Gramophone Company has recorded the whole play, allowing us to be quite independent of theatres. The vocal parts were taken by competent artists and the whole fantasy sounds, we think, just as Elgar would have conceived it. It is another case in which we have to be thankful for the composer's insight into the gramophone possibilities. The outline of the recording, which constitutes an album of records, is here given :—

"THE STARLIGHT EXPRESS"
(Sir Edward Elgar, O.M.)

(Orchestra Personally Conducted by the Composer.)
12-inch records 6s.

02639   The Organ Grinder's Songs. No. 1. "To the Children" (Charles Mott) (78)

02640   The Organ Grinder's Songs. No. 2. "The Blue-Eyes Fairy" (Charles Mott) (78)

02641   The Organ Grinder's Songs. No. 3. "My Old Tunes" (Charles Mott) (78)

02642   "Curfew Song" (Orion) (Charles Mott) (78)

02643   (a) Song—" Come Little Winds " (Charles
            Mott)

        (b) Wind Dance (Orchestra)

03472   (a) Tears and Laughter (Agnes Nicholls) (78)

        (b) Sunrise Song (Agnes Nicholls) (78)

03473   The Laugher's Song (Agnes Nicholls) (78)

04151   Finale—" Hearts Must be Soft-Shiny Dressed"
            (Agnes Nicholls and Charles Mott) (78)

The figures in brackets at end of selections indicate
the speed at which the records should be played.

The songs now available are those of the *Organ
Grinder* in the fantasy. No. 1 is *To The Children*,
No. 2 *The Blue-Eyes Fairy* and No. 3 *My Old Tunes*.
These are absolutely three of the most charming songs
by Elgar.   They are full of youthful melody and have
a peculiar, distinctive appeal which prevents us from
calling to mind any others with which they may be
compared.

The most important key to the whole is, as we have
noticed, the *Pianoforte Suite*. This consists of six
numbers arranged by the capable Ketelby. The
technical requirements are within reach of the ordinary
amateur, but the pianist who has not the album in
his *repertoire* has missed some of the most charming
and original music of modern times.

No. 1. *To The Children* (*Organ Grinder's Song*).
It is fitting that the first number should be inscribed

to the youngsters, for it is their ideas that dominate the play. The piece opens with two bars of rocking accompaniment, over which an innocent little theme is constructed. Soon another light-hearted little melody occurs and after a playful variation, the more serious Elgar prevails. A reference to the opening *moderato* leads to a repetition of the *Allegretto* and its sprightly capers. The innocent opening theme is heard again and concludes on a trill which leads to an original *coda* of five bars of the very essence of youthful happiness.

No. 2. *Dance of the Pleiades*. This is one of those lovely and expressive gems that Elgar sometimes indulges in. An introduction of four bars is built on an idea of beautiful contemplation. The dance commences in 12–8 time and is at once graceful and charming, and the middle section consists of a sprightly idea in thirds, the rhythm of which was employed with delightful effect in the fifth of the *Enigma Variations* (Op. 36). After this charming and contrasting idea has been dwelt on, the first dance theme returns.

No. 3. *Sunrise Song*. This is very short and its thematic material consists of one idea only. The solitary theme, however, has a great amount of vivacity and the number is notable for its brilliant, engaging rhythm.

No. 4. *In the Forest*. This opens *Molto moderato* with an expressive and quiet suggestion of the silence of the forest. Soon a typical Elgarian melody enters, *Lento* (*pp espress*) ; it is exceedingly simple, but none the less impressive. The air will be recognised as the middle section from the *Fairy Pipers* number of the first *Wand of Youth* suite. It is immediately followed by the forest theme, and after a time a simple, but impressive and typical climax is reached. The piece concludes with further references to the borrowed theme being heard *ppp*, high in the scale followed by a running crochet figure of secondary importance.

No. 5. *The Blue-Eyes Fairy* (*Organ-Grinder's Song*). This is a valse and has met with some popularity. It opens with some decisive chords, after which the valse theme is announced. It has the true rhythm that sets the listener unconsciously in motion. In parts we notice the stronger Elgarian element, but the piece is chiefly noticeable as an example of what a serious master may do with the " popular " type of music. We much prefer this valse by Elgar to the many trashy specimens extant by people who do nothing else but write " hunnybug " airs. Concerning the main melody the *Daily News* critic remarked that it " will haunt the memory for many a day."

No. 6. *Finale.* The last number opens with a soft reiteration of the dominant. At the second bar a typical idea enters and has an equally typical from of progression, culminating with an impressive *allargando*, the most striking we have heard in this

suite as regards nobleness and the greater Elgar
It is immediately followed by the expressive air of the
middle section of *Little Bells* (*Scherzando*) from the
second *Wand of Youth* suite. After a time a broad
and obviously orchestral passage is reached and soon
a series of *tremolo* chords lead to another theme
(*Grandioso*). This is given out *fortissimo* in the bass
and continued in the treble. The tune, which is
presented with thunderous effect, will be recognised
as that of the familiar hymn, *The First Noel.* After
this the *Little Bells* theme is heard with an appropriate
accompaniment in the form of a peal of bells. This
new effect soon assumes the principle part, the *finale*
concluding with the bells being thundered out in
octaves. At the last bar, however, they have died
away to *pianissimo*, the *finale* chord being accompanied by a deep, indefinite roll on the tonic.

The ideal of the whole suite is charm and happiness
without frivolity, for Elgar's character was too strong
to be tainted by the general light play of the theatre
and his fantasy preserves the spirit of genuine musicianship. The whole contains entrancing music, but
so unmistakably the work of a serious man and so
different to the typical modern play that chases the
public ear with short-lived Americanisms.

OPUS 79. RECITATION WITH MUSIC, " LE DRAPEAU BELGE " (" THE BELGIAN FLAG ").

The huge success of *Carillon* evidently tempted the composer to write another work on the same subject. *The Belgian Flag*, however, while a meritorious and really interesting work, has never attained the popularity of its great predecessor. *Carillon* is international in spirit and appeals to everyone with a sense of deeper patriotism. The later work revolves in a much smaller sphere, possessing no great attractions apart from its immediate object ; it is not therefore surprising that it is overshadowed by its greater relative.

OPUS 80. CHORAL WORK, FOR TENOR OR SOPRANO SOLO, CHORUS, ORCHESTRA AND ORGAN, " THE SPIRIT OF ENGLAND."

Composed in 1915. First Movement appeared in the Summer, 1917. Second and Third Movements in Spring, 1916.

" *My Portion of this Work I Humbly Dedicate to the Memory of Our Glorious Men, with a Special Thought for the Worcesters. Edward Elgar, 1915.*"

No. 1. *The Fourth of August.*   No. 2. *To Women.*
No. 3. *For the Fallen.*

From Laurence Binyon's *The Winnowing Fan.*

This is not only the greatest of Elgar's " Great-War " productions, but one of his finest and noblest

choral works. The spirit of humanity breathes
throughout the piece, for the composer had by this
time realised the true significance of the ghastly war.
There is no Boer War martial spirit in this work,
instead there is the greater message of the crusade of
freedom. Elgar saw the efforts of his countrymen,
their sacrifices, and in this insight is the essence of the
work. The composer felt with the people and in
consequence *The Spirit of England* is an expression
of the nobler feelings of the whole nation in the time of
bitterness and trial. We may turn to it and find our
deepest emotions—sorrow, love and pride—voiced by
one who felt it all. Out of this comes the sick loathing
with which the nation regarded and still regards the
militarist promoters of " Kultur." This, too, we find
expressed in the work, for the composer can only
conceive the *Gerontius* (Op. 38) theme of the *Demons*,
howling outside the Judgment Hall, as fit for the
German Junker.

1. *The Fourth of August* reminds us of the days
when we took up our tiny weapons to save ourselves
from the future greed of the oppressor. The seriousness of the times are expressed throughout, although
the spirit of freedom rings out loud and clear. As we
have already noticed, the theme of the *Demons Chorus*
is here made symbolic of their earthly equivalents.
The very idea that Newman described as like a panto-
mime, is here used with great significance and as the
full force of the German Imperialists' character dawns

upon the composer, the music increases in intensity.

Apart from the necessary unsavoryness, however, the dominant note is one of spiritual hope and encouragement.

2. *To Women.* This strikes a solemn note at first, for the poem tells of women's lot. The bravest women of all being those who endured in silence the alternate love and anguish. No outward glory was there for them, but only the sobbing pride of sacrifice or the agony of long suspense.

The silent victory of the greater women who stayed at home truly inspired Elgar to his greatest efforts. The chief sentiments of the number are those of brooding, but there often comes the light of spiritual comfort.

3. *For the Fallen.* This number commences with a solemn and impressive theme and soon assumes a deep sadness, vivid in its expressiveness. Above the whole there floats a proud feeling that is immediately grasped by the mind, but which is difficult to describe. At times it is boldly at the fore, at others it is hushed by the lament, but we are always conscious of this underlying power. The whole mood of the number, however, is of cherished remembrance of those who gave their lives and hopes in the hope that we might exist in freedom. Near the end the music bursts out loud and clear, but the stirring strains die away to quiet resignation and hope for the future.

The Spirit of England will go down to posterity as one of the greatest memorials of greater England.

For those who desire closer acquaintance with it, the vocal score, which is listed at half-a-crown, will be found a fine study. Any of the numbers may be performed separately.

OPUS 81. BALLET, " THE FAN."

Produced Solely for the Benefit of a War Charity and Only Performed at the Chelsea Palace in 1917.

The career of the *Fan Ballet* opened and closed with its production All that now remains extant is a pianoforte arrangement of the *Echo's Dance.* This is, however, an exceedingly pleasing piece, and while being of no great mechanical difficulty to the performer, requires a minute and musicianly attention to the phrasing and tone-colour. The composer has given implicit directions for its performance and, properly conceived as regards delicacy of expression, the piece is not at all uninteresting. The sentiments do not run very deep and the Elgarian phrases which will be at once noticed are only surface effects, but they undoubtedly impart a dignity to the whole.

OPUS 82. SONATA IN E MINOR, FOR VIOLIN
AND PIANOFORTE.

First Produced at the Second Meeting of the British
Music Society, London Centre, on March 13th, 1919.
Played by W. H. Reed and Anthony Bernard.

First Public Performance, March 21st, 1919, at a
Chamber Concert (British String Quartet). Played
by W. H. Reed and Landon Ronald.

Dedicated to M. J., 1918.

1. *Allegro* (*Risoluto*).
2. *Romanze* (*Andante*).
3. *Finale* (*Allegro*).

The announcement that Elgar had turned his
attention to chamber music in three forms, a *Sonata*
for violin and pianoforte, a *String Quartet*, and a
Quintet for pianoforte and strings, aroused widespread
interest at the time.

The *Sonata*, which appeared first, was hailed as a
monumental addition to the already flourishing school
of English chamber music, but there were some who
expected something of the magnitude of the symphonies and were disappointed. Now the striking
point about the *Sonata* is its conciseness ; there is

little or nothing of an epoch-making work in it. Elgar delayed his published chamber music till late in life, but the first example was direct and bore no deep problem. The great achievements were the reviving of the classical form and the perfected condensement of material, so lacking in the *symphonies* and *violin concerto*. There is not a bar of superfluous matter, such as may be found in the larger works mentioned.

The *Violin Sonata* is not the first attempt of its kind by Elgar, for it is well known that his manuscripts contain many examples of chamber music; Opus 9, it may be remembered, in a *Violin Sonata*. Op. 82, however, is the first example Elgar thought worthy of his powers.

The first public performance of the *E minor Sonata* was particularly striking owing to Landon Ronald being at the pianoforte, but we naturally enjoyed the interpretation of W. H. Reed. The *Sonata* was soon played all over England with success, for it is full of interest both to players and audience.

A vital factor of the work is its striving after something greater. The apparent disappointment of those who expected a great work is due to the fact that Elgar had some great object in mind which was not realised in the first attempt. A close study of the *Sonata* reveals, beyond the contrasting elements, of vigour and contemplative beauty, a depth that cannot be easily ignored. An apparent foreshadowing of greater things to come is often evident, but a realisation does not seem to be affected. The general character of the *Sonata* is lucid, animated at times by much vigour, but always tempered by the beautiful. As a single work, we feel the piece to be a fine and spirited example, but its true significance lies in its foreshadowing of the immortal *Quintet*. This crowning achievement is singularly separated from the present work, however, by the quartet, an altogether pyschologically different masterpiece.

It is hardly necessary to emphasise the brilliance with which Elgar treats the violin, but his pianoforte writing, by reason of its scarcity, gives occasion for discussion. We may say at once, that it is not really pure treatment. The composer seems to miss the colour resources of the orchestra and in consequence the pianoforte often sounds suspiciously like one engaged with an orchestral transcription.

1. The *Allegro* opens with a vigorous theme and is naturally followed by a contrasting one. The remaining part of the movement contains some typically Elgarian ideas, including a mysterious atmosphere and finally concludes with a stirring *Coda*.

2. The *Romance* commences with solemn strains, conveying an impression of profound gravity. We should like to know what this opening means, for it is widely different to the main melody, which is one of idyllic charm. Elgar has always made the slow

movement the most expressive and auto-biographical, but in the present work, under the influence of the dreamy theme, the whole atmosphere becomes wrapped in filmy beauty. After a time, however, the meditations unfold and an intense climax is reached. It is as if the musings were gradually illuminated until at length their significance dazzles the whole community of ideas. The first section returns with the violin muted and in the original mood the movement ends.

3. The *Finale* commences with a broad tune, but the emotions are ever the master and the movement resolves itself into a veritable wealth of passionate sentiments. The culmination comes with a lofty climax at a height attained by few other composers. The work ends in a superb and ennobling spirit of triumph.

We cannot help repeating that the *Sonata* is an exceptionally fine work indeed, but Elgar's standard had by this time become so high that exceptional greatness was looked for in each new work. It said much for the *Sonata* when the musical world accorded it as being worthy of the composer.

The score of the work bears the inscription, " Brinkwells, 1918."

OPUS 83. QUARTET IN E MINOR, FOR STRINGS.

First Produced at an Invitation Concert at Leo F. Schuster's House, Westminster, London, on May 3rd, 1919.

First Performed in Public at an Elgar Chamber Concert on May 21st, 1919, at Wigmore Hall, London.

Played by Albert Sammons (First Violin), W. H. Reed (Second Violin), Raymond Jeremy (Viola), and Felix Salmond ('Cello).

Dedicated to the Brodsky Quartet.

No. 1 *Allegro Moderato.*

No. 2. *Piacevole (Poco Andante).*

No. 3. *Finale (Allegro Molto).*

The *String Quartet* (Op. 83) is one of the most unique of Elgar's works. Throughout it is of refreshing beauty and always original. It is at all times invigorating and although possessing passages of surpassing loveliness, the atmosphere is never heavy. The composer sought to refrain from dwelling on beautiful ideas, the result being a particularly interesting work and another example of Elgar's ability to invigorate a well-worn form with health. The *Quartet* found great favour with press and public

on its production, because of its pleasing character.
There are no dark or underlying problems, its beauty
is natural, and its vigour direct. We should not
deem it a grand and noble work like the *Pianoforte
Quintet*, but it stands alone as Elgar's most pastoral
essay. There are, it is true, many brilliant and fiery
passages in the work, but it is significant of its general
character that the indication *Nobilmente* occurs only
once. The sole occasion occurs near the end of the
first movement ; its loftiness is apparent and forms
one of the strongest passages in the work.

It is a happy fact that Elgar's three great chamber
works, Op. 82, 83 and 84, were purely native products.
They are directly connected with a lovely little corner
of Sussex and reflect the pastoral atmosphere of this
charming county. The *Quartet* especially would
appear to be a reflection of the English countryside ;
by it we are more than ever convinced that English
chamber music is the finest in the world. When we
recollect the *Quartet in D* of J. D. Davis, the *Peter
Pan* of Walford Davies, the chamber music by John
Ireland, York Bowen, Stanford, Frank Bridge, Waldo
Warner, J. B. McEwen and others, the examples of
Mendelssohn, Schumann and Brahms appear to be
stodgy and laboured ; even Beethoven is not so
pleasing after some of the English works in this
sphere and Schubert alone seems to be beautiful.
Now that Elgar's chamber music is added to the
list of native examples, we may find all that is needed

in our own composers. The quality of the music is always high, for it has been greatly encouraged by generous prize givers, and the volume of tone obtained from the strings is really superior to anything the classics obtained. It is only to a few modern foreign composers that we look for anything to compare with the chamber music of the English writers mentioned above.

1. The first movement, 12-8 time, commences with a seriousness that warns off any who may doubt its lofty inspiration. Commencing *piano*, in the second bar it has reached a *sforzando*, the effect of which at once signifies the energy of the composer. The third bar (*espress*) sees the commencement of a typical Elgarian element that runs through the *Allegro*. The downward leaping fourths will play an important part as it proceeds and, with the answering ascending figure, the idea forms the basis of the greater part of this movement. It is another example of how some of the greatest works spring from apparently tiny ideas. The whole of the *Quartet* we are dealing with contains figures that are quite straightforward, yet the net result is a masterpiece.

As the movement unfolds we cannot fail to be impressed by the volume of tone which the composer draws from the instruments. The variety of moods, *allargando, stringendo, espress con fuoco, nobilmente*, all keep the players in constant animation. Although the second subject is quiet and thoughtful, the

N

dominant mood of the movement is a seeking after
something ; an apparent quest for explanation and
satisfaction. The end comes softly, with a reminiscence of the opening figure.

2. The slow movement is one of the loveliest things
Elgar ever composed and was much favoured by his
wife. The simple charm and innocence of its opening
creates a wonderful effect of tranquility. The
second violin, viola and 'cello alone are at first engaged,
the first violin not entering until the 23rd bar and
then only to double the second for thirteen measures.
The movement is in 3-8 time and proceeds along in
complete contentment. Particularly happy are the
harmonious little imitations among the instruments.
After a time some striking *pizzicato* passages are heard
and soon the first subject returns *fortissimo* (*espress*).
A rather fanciful effect catches our attention. The
second violins and viola give out the melody an
octave apart while the first violin has an upper C.
The latter instrument, as if protesting against its
premiership not being recognised, emphatically gives
out the third bar of the theme before the other two
have reached it. Their statement is therefore made
to sound little more than an echo, for the first violin
made it clear that the early notes were something
more than an anticipation. Throughout this incident
the 'cello maintains a dignified neutrality.

The music now proceeds along the formal route
until the *Coda* is reached. In this, familiar devises

of the composer are brought to play and the movement ends softly on the tonic chord.

4. The *Finale* opens *risoluto*, 4-4 time. From the first its vivacious character is evident. The players now seem more busy and we are again impressed with the volume of sound proceeding from only four instruments. It is not absolutely necessary here to dwell on the various themes of this movement, but there is no mistaking the general policy. The first subject is brilliant and animated ; the second is indicated *dolce*. The whole affords a most invigorating and welcome *Finale* to the music we have already heard. Elgar has let himself go with the bounding energy of the natural atmosphere, and were it not for this relaxation which he always brought into his large works, we should become jaded with the very beauty of their expressions. The composer felt the effects of the work beforehand, for even pastoral serenity must have an antidote. The *finale* movement, while tempered with expressive passages, abounds with life and activity which, some pages from the end, completely dominates the whole. The conclusion comes with a magnificent *fortissimo*.

As in the case of the *Violin Sonata* (Op. 83), the end of the *Quartet* bears the inscription, " Brinkwells, 1918."

OPUS 84. QUINTET IN A MINOR, FOR PIANOFORTE AND STRINGS.

First Produced at an Invitation Concert at Leo F. Schuster's House, Westminster, London, on May 3rd, 1919.

First Performed in Public on May 21st, 1919, in MS., at the Wigmore Hall, London.

Played by William Murdoch (Pianoforte), Albert Sammons (First Violin), W. H. Reed (Second Violin), Raymond Jeremy (Viola) and Felix Salmond (Violoncello).

Dedicated to Ernest Newman.

We now come upon one of Elgar's most powerful works and a masterpiece of great significance. The *Quintet* is the culmination of the composer's sudden attention to serious chamber music. It has a depth of remarkable proportions, a wealth of romantic colour and ennobling spiritual power. The slow movement is one of the greatest and most moving that we have heard and time alone will decide whether it is not the summit of Elgar's *Adagios*, the medium through which he expressed his thoughts in the most human and appealing manner. More even than this, the whole work is like nothing in significance that the composer had written before. Like the *Ninth Sym-*

phony of Beethoven it shows a great stride forward, towards some great and unknown goal. It is in no spirit of rhapsody that we impress upon the reader the importance of this *Quintet*. There are passages in it where an altogether new Elgar is found. A greater, although not necessarily finer, Elgar even than the one of the *symphonies* and *violin concertos*. In the present work he more than ever strives to break away from the course followed for so many years; there are even obvious indications of the effort with which the desire to dwell on beautiful thoughts is forsaken. In all the movements we discern a greater Elgar, with some of the grim strength of Beethoven. It was not to be expected, of course, that a complete change of character would take place in one who was so distinctive in style. The work is at once Elgarian in certain of its themes and in one lovely passage we can easily recall the Southern warmth of *In the South*. What we wish to emphasise is the appearance of the colossal. The loveliness only appears to temper the underlying power. There is more iron in the present work than in any of its predecessors; altogether its significance is great and extremely difficult to measure.

1. The first movement may be regarded as the first expression of a certain great inspiration, for the *Quintet* is, like its big forerunners, a unified whole. The remaining two movements serve to expound more fully and perhaps more nobly, this unknown ideal.

The work opens *Moderato* in soft, but nevertheless decisive tones, given out by the pianoforte. This is followed by a pleading phrase for the strings. The composer does not dwell long on these somewhat enigmatic utterings and the typically vigorous *Allegro* soon establishes itself. The animation of this theme culminates in a passage marked *Con fuoco*, prominent in which is the opening idea of the pianoforte. A period of silence intervenes between this stirring passage and the entry of a quieter section, led by the opening phrase of the second idea of the *Moderato*. Soon a passage occurs dearly beloved by chamber-music audiences. It has a romantic warmth of the Southern variety, so exquisitely used in the concert-overture, *In the South* (Op. 50).

The passage referred to is prepared for by a charming and expressively delicate episode in A major. The theme itself, however, is in the dominant of this key, but the modulation is hardly noticed.

An idea so expressively Elgarian and which has so taken the fancy of Elgarites, must be quoted :—

Of great importance to the analyst, but of little consequence to the sheer lover of music, is the fact that it forms the second subject of the movement.

The composer dwells on it for some time, using lovely tone-colour, till the atmosphere becomes more clouded and from now onwards, we must pass through passages of varied and intricate skill ; music, indeed, that describes itself independently of literary versions.

The recapitulation in its technical aspect is completely overshadowed by the power of emotion. In it the movement reaches its spiritual idea. The themes reappear in gorgeous colour and beautiful sentiment, and it seems almost superfluous to point out the immense variety of contrast in all forms. The perfect realm of Elgar is found here and the significance of this need not be expounded to readers of *this* book.

The movement ultimately ends *pianissimo*, despite an attempt to provide a dramatic close.

2. The *Adagio* of this work is one of the most penetrating and moving of its kind. Elgar was particularly successful with the slow movement and in the present example his appeal goes straight to the soul of the listener. We do not hesitate to place it beside the great *Adagio* of the *A flat Symphony*, for its message is as compelling even as that phenominal example. Its sincerity and depth need not be hampered with analytical considerations, for they are the factors which enable it to stand high in the estimation of all who hear it.

MAIN THEME OF THE ADAGIO.

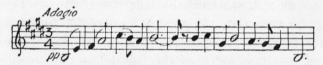

3. The *Finale* commences *Andante*, the subject matter being taken from the phrase for strings in the opening *Moderato*. The *Allegro* itself commences *con dignita* and is of strong character. After this has been dwelt on, culminating, it must be noticed, in a passage marked *Nobilmente* and dying away high in the strings, the second subject enters. Its swaying rhythm is contrasting to the decisive character of its predecessor, and its whole being is controlled by an apparently nervous force.

After a time a new figure of much greater animation enters and from this we proceed to the middle section. In this many familiar themes are heard, or to be more expressive, seen through the hazy beauty of the whole. This atmosphere is only dispelled by the reappearance of the *Allegro*, strong even in its new and subdued version. The music from this point to the end gradually grows in strength and brilliance. It shows, perhaps, more vividly than any other section of the work, the essential unity of the whole. We do not obtain this view merely because of the presence of familiar themes, but from the general impression of the whole work.

The end comes in a blaze of light, the nervous figure

being prominent in its *Grandioso* aspect and also the strong *Allegro*, which has the last triumphal word.

So ends this, the greatest example of Elgar's remarkable chamber music. Of the music itself we have of course spoken; of the instrumentation we need say nothing, it is from Elgar; of the spiritual message we cannot speak definitely; it has a singular appeal, but that powerful, almost insinuous enigmatic feature of Elgar allows us no psychological key to the whole.

Like the two preceding works, the *Quintet* bears the inscription, " Brinkwells, 1918."

OPUS 85. CONCERTO IN E MINOR, FOR VIOLONCELLO AND ORCHESTRA.

First Performed in Public, October 27th, 1919, at the Queen's Hall, London.

Soloist, Felix Salmond. London Symphony Orchestra Conducted by the Composer.

Dedicated to Sidney and Frances Colvin.

No. 1. *Recit. Adagio-Moderato.*
No. 2. *Allegro Molto.*
No. 3. *Adagio.*
No. 4. *Allegro non Troppo.*

Elgar realised a wish of some years' existence when he wrote the *'Cello Concerto*. The work was composed in the summer preceding its production and naturally reflects the English countryside where it was written. At first hearing the work appears to be decidedly dull in many places, for we are unconsciously comparing it with the kindred large works, more especially the *Concerto for Violin*. The true light, however, is that given forth by Elgar's later period, which was expounded clearly in the striking chamber music group. In consequence therefore, the rich and decorative elements give way to a deeper and more concentrated terseness ; a more simple, yet greater current of beauty and a less complicated mode of exposition, born of greater wisdom and deeper insight.

The chief technical concern of the composer was the interweaving of the solo and orchestral parts. The range and *timbre* of the 'cello calls for extremely careful consideration in the writing of a *concerto* for it and Elgar's orchestration therefore is deprived of its usual richness, more especially as the solo instrument is almost continuously employed. The outbursts of tone in *tutti* passages of the *Violin Concerto* are conspicuous by their scarcity in the present work.

The whole aspect of the *'Cello Concerto* is generally tranquil, yet it is obviously inspired by the deepest feelings of humanity. There is no occasion for external display, the whole work is indicative of earnestness and a wistful realisation of life's beauties. It is an extremely sensitive recording of the composer's later mentality ; there is no thought or claim for popularity, but there is understanding in it for all of us who look out on life in an æsthetical, yet problematical sense.

1. The *Concerto* opens with a short *recitative* for the soloist. The emotional aspect is at once serious and expressive of the term *Nobilmente*, which is prefixed to the score. The ensuing *moderato* presents a more pastoral character, which is, however, strongly romantic and inclined to be mysterious.

After some repetitions, a new idea enters. It is more possessing in appearance and decidedly welcome. The whole soon becomes serious, the 'cello having passages of impassioned thoughtfulness. Finally the first theme reappears and the movement dies softly away. There is no break between this movement and the next.

2. A few introductory bars for the soloist and also some awakening *pizzicati* from the orchestra usher in the *scherzando*-like theme, the chief feature and effect of which is the reiterated note idea..

Soon a change of mood is expressed in a lovely *cantabile* melody, embraced by both soloist and orchestra. The soothing calmness of this new theme is felt to the end of the movement, even through the liveliness of the foregoing melody, which of course returns with all its vivacity.

3. The slow movement of an Elgar work always arouses within us the thoughts of exquisite beauty and penetrating emotion. In the present work it

comes as a pure song-like uttering, the climax of the spiritual attitude presented to us at the opening bars of the work. It is one comparatively short flow of lyrical beauty, from which no definite melody may easily be plucked. The air is at first tranquil, but soon the expressive strains of the solo instrument prepare for the broadening out, which culminates in a superbly emotional climax. The calmer mood, however, returns and continues to the end of the movement, which is a very mirror of the new Elgar. It proceeds without a break into the *Finale*.

4. The opening *recitative* appears again at the commencement of the *Finale* but now more powerful in appearance. The principal theme soon enters and is at once strong and quasi-humorous. After some discussion of this, the second subject appears and this in turn leads to a *bravura* passage for the solo 'cello. The latter occasion is an exceptional one and a concession by the composer.

The first theme now reappears in unified 'cellos, later augmented by the double-basses. It is still further expounded by the full orchestra. The second theme also reappears and is subjected to some of the familiar orchestral tints of Elgar. The music becomes calmer, but the *Coda* brings a sudden change. The solo 'cello gives out a striking phrase and the whole becomes intense, almost despairing in quality. The restful mood returns, however, and with it there soon come the serious tones of the opening *recitative*.

A final statement of the principle subject is made in an impressive manner and the work ends with loud, decisive chords.

The 'Cello Concerto is a fine work of art, but it is more important as an insight into the finer spirit of the later Elgar. To some it may actually appear a dull work and as far as external decorations are concerned it is comparatively so, but we are not so much concerned with this aspect when a greater one is before us. We remember too, that with the exception of the " popular " works, Elgar has always written for the intellectual ; not necessarily for the cultivated, but for the æsthetical mind, the mind that goes through life as an onlooker in addition to something that participates in its essential joys and sorrows. It is in this direction that we believe Elgar's Violoncello Concerto is supreme ; it is a more intimate reflection of the later manhood than its predecessors and in consequence it has less covering. It is a momentous exposition rather than a gorgeous musical work ; a study for the prober more than a feast for the lover.

There is, of course, much that may be termed " fine music " and the work must be given much credit on this score. The themes are interesting and straightforward and the whole Concerto is not too long, suggesting that Elgar remembered that the length of some of his previous works were obstacles to their appreciation and performance.

We are impressed with this musical value, for
'cello *concertos* are liable to oppressiveness, and consider it, in its directness, to be well worthy of the
composer and satisfying to the average concert
audience. It is imperative, however, that the period-
ical development of Elgar should be familiar to the
listener before he claims to give an opinion of the
work. More than this, we think it is necessary that
he should feel intimately the personal character of
Elgar in its various stages of development. Without this it is no more possible to appreciate the inner
significance of the *Concerto*, than it is to understand
the last *Pianoforte Sonata* of Beethoven without having
first made the acquaintance, and felt the development through, the preceding ones. Even a fancied
understanding is not convincing enough.

The first public performance of the *Concerto* was
enthusiastically received, the composer being greeted
on appearance with cheers. The presentation, however, was not satisfactory, for it was marked by lack
of unity in the orchestra, with consequent loss of
effects. Further performances happily presented the
work in a better light. Thus was another Elgar work
launched upon its career, proving that with advancing
age the composer's spiritual and technical thoughts
were as convincing and progressive as ever. The less
imposing, but greater and more ideal power of *Nobilmente* is seen for the first time.

WORKS WITHOUT OPUS NUMBERS.

SERENADE LYRIQUE, FOR ORCHESTRA.

This is one of Elgar's early works, composed before he began Opus numbering. It is notable for its marked individuality and although a rather ordinary type of piece, it has as its main theme an unmistakable Elgarian melody.

The middle section is rather interesting, but the whole aspect of the work is dominated by a genuine desire, and even power, to create musical expression. The Elgar of the *Serenade Lyrique* is as sincere in his comparative crudeness as the Elgar of the *Violin Concerto* in his sublime maturity. The little piece has nothing to compare with the two pieces without Opus number composed in the composer's later years, but the sentiments of the delightful *Carissima* and *Rosemary* may easily be traced to it. The work makes an effective pianoforte solo and, under Margaret Fairless, a very expressive violin solo.

" CARISSIMA," FOR ORCHESTRA.

This is one of Elgar's prettiest pieces, being of the *Salut D'Amour* type. It possesses the true Elgar spirit, rising at times to a really ennobling outburst. Although a light work, it shows the hand of the great composer and is essentially a little masterpiece. Its arrangements for home use are justified by the pleasing results.

" ROSEMARY," FOR ORCHESTRA.

Like *Carissima*, this piece is of the *Salut D'Amour* type. It is very charming indeed and strengthened in places by the greater Elgar. These two pieces without Opus number are trifles, but they are trifles of the great composer and must be taken into account.

SONGS WITH ORCHESTRA, " THE FRINGES OF THE FLEET."

Produced at the Coliseum, London, in June, 1917, running Daily until August of the same Year, under the Composer's Baton.

Performed by Charles Mott, Harry Barratt, Frederick Henry and Frederick Stewart.

Words by Rudyard Kipling.

Dedicated to Admiral Lord Beresford.

The Fringes of the Fleet are by far the most important of Elgar's works without Opus number. They comprise some of the most popular music of the day, but nevertheless, are worthy to be ranked with the composer's other fine works.

There is no mistaking the breezy atmosphere of the whole, while the sentiments are always stirring and savour of the national spirit of English seamen. Altogether we consider them, both as regards words and music, a noble tribute to those noble men, the merchant seamen of the European War period.

No. 1. *The Lowestoft Boat.*

" In Lowestoft a boat was laid,
　Mark well what I do say !
And she was built for the herring trade,
　But she has gone a-rovin', a-rovin', a rovin',
　The Lord knows where ! "

The first verse of this song gives the key to its character, the lines going on to describe how the fishing boat on war service prowled about the North Sea with her humorous crew, the leading lights of the party being characteristically described. The music is very breezy and the words " a-rovin' " are brought out with seamen's hearty jocularity. In the original production, the curtain rose on typical scenery, with four artists in rough-and-ready merchant-seamen's clothes, seated round an equally rough-and-ready table. The original caste has been recorded by the Gramophone Company.

O

No. 2. *Fate's Discourtesy*. This number retains the salty atmosphere and we may again reproduce some lines to indicate the character of words and music :—

" Be well assured that on our side
  Our challenged oceans fight,
Though headlong wind and heaping tide
  Make us their sport to-night.

No. 3. *Submarines*. The character of this number is intensely dramatic and gripping when the actions of the artists are inspired. It is the shortest of the four songs, but not the least interesting. The setting of the last two lines :—

" And the mirth of a seaport dies
  When our blow gets home,"

is very impressive.

No. 4. *The Sweepers*.

" Dawn off the Foreland—the young flood making
  Jumbled and short and steep—
Black in the hollows and bright where it's breaking—
  Awkward water to sweep.
  " Mines reported in the fairway,
    Warn all traffic and detain.
  'Sent up *Unity*, *Claribel*, *Assyrian*,
    Stormcock, and *Golden Gain*."

This opens quietly, but very bustling and important are the mine-sweepers. In each verse, and there are three, the nautical spirit is heightened by the sounding of a bell. The whole of this number is very breezy and genuinely British in sentiment.

The *Fringes of the Fleet* have worthily attained a place among Elgar's music. The composer caught the spirit of the lines in a typical British manner and after these songs the belief, which was well founded, that Elgar would always be regarded as cosmopolitan, was dropped. While this statement will always apply to his large symphonic works, the songs we are dealing with will stand as a proof of Elgar's British spirit.

There are a number of other pieces by Elgar which do not bear an Opus number. They are not of great importance, except the songs which we will give afterwards. We will now mention some various instrumental pieces which we came across in our travels for information.

ASCHERBERG, HOPWOOD AND CREW have a piece entitled *Bizarrerie* in their albums as a violin solo and also for pianoforte solo. This piece is interesting and although an early work, bears much that is typical and foreshadowing of the greater Elgar. In a pianoforte album entitled *A Score of Romantic Fragments*, Volume I., there is an *Idylle* by Elgar. The piece pleased us very much, in fact, the whole album is attractive, containing light works by Edward German, Grieg, Tchaikovski, Arensky, Liszt, Moszkovsik, Paderevski and others.

ORGAN PIECES. *Moderato. Allegretto.* Contained in an Organ Album (Music Lovers' Library).

SONGS NOT MENTIONED BEFORE IN THIS BOOK :—

An interesting album contains seven songs by Elgar, entitled :—

1. *Like to the Damask Rose.* 2. *Queen Mary's Song.* 3. *A Song of Autumn.* 4. *A Poet's Life.* 5. *Thro' the Long Days.* 6. *Ronde'.* 7. *The Shepherd's Song.*

SONGS FROM BOOSEY AND CO.'S CATALOGUE.

EDWARD ELGAR.

After	F, G, & A
Always and Everywhere	G
Arabian Serenade	G minor
Chariots of the Lord (The)	C, D♭, D, & E♭
Come, Gentle Night ..	C, D. & E♭
In the Dawn	C, E♭, & E
Is She Not Passing Fair ? ..	D, F, & G
King's Way (The) ..	F, G, & A♭

(Chorus part in O.N. or Sol-fa, each price 1d.)
(Organ Accomp., price 6d. ; Chorus part, 1d.
Unison and S.A.T.B., in Old Notation and Tonic Sol-fa).

Works Without Numbers

Pipes of Pan (The)	..	G, A, & B
(Organ Accomp., price 6d.)		
Song of Flight (A)	..	A♭
Speak, Music	.. ..	A, B♭, & C
Speak, My Heart	.. ..	C
War Song (A)	.. ..	C & D
Wind at Dawn (The)	..	F

Inside the Bar. (ENOCH AND SONS). This song is after the style of the Fleet Songs and is worthy of attention. It is in four parts, unaccompanied.

VOCAL MUSIC PUBLISHED BY NOVELLO AND CO. NOT MENTIONED BEFORE IN THIS BOOK :—

Follow the Colours. Marching Song for Soldiers. Words by Captain W. de Courcy Stretton. This is an exceedingly healthy song, eminently suitable for a marching body.

God Save the King. (Arranged for Chorus and Orchestra). This is really a fine version of the English national anthem and very successful. The vocal score is listed at threepence.

A Child Asleep. Song for contralto.

PART-SONGS. The appended list contains interesting and effective examples of Elgar's part-songs. A form of music which we have seen he wrote with considerable scholarliness and expression, and in which he attained great popularity among choral societies :—*The Birthright,* Marching Song ; *My Love Dwelt in a Northern Land, How Calmly the Evening, Evening Scene.*

PART-SONGS WITH GERMAN WORDS :—*Romanze* (*Im Norden, wo mein Lieb gewohnt*). *Tief birgt mein Herz.*

ANTHEMS :—*Fear Not, O Lord* (Harvest), *Lo! Christ the Lord is Born* (Carol), *O Mightiest of the Mighty* (Coronation Hymn), *They are at Rest* (Elegy).

With Proud Thanksgiving. This is an arrangement from *For the Fallen* (*The Spirit of England,* Op. 80) made at the request of the League of Arts, to whom it is dedicated. It was specially intended to be performed at the Dedication of the Cenotaph, London, which was erected in memory of those who fell in the European War, and also at similar ceremonies in other parts of the country. Needless to say its stirring sentiments make it an extremely impressive part of such ceremonies, whether in the open air or not. The work is for S.A.T.B. chorus, with accompaniment for military or brass band, or for organ or pianoforte.

CONTEMPORARY BOOKS ON ELGAR.

This List is Exclusive of Articles in Newspapers, Magazines, etc.

BUCKLEY, R. J. *Sir Edward Elgar.* Living Masters of Music Series. Published by John Lane, The Bodley Head, Vigo Street, London, W.1., and New York, U.S.A. Edited by Rosa Newmarch. Price 2s.6d. net.

This book is biographical and its present edition does not extend beyond the year 1904. The greatest events in Elgar's life are for the most part, therefore, not included. The work, however, is of great interest owing to the author's familiarity with Elgar and because of the sincerity of his writing. We ourselves learnt much from it and commend it as indispensable to every Elgar lover.

NEWMAN, ERNEST. *Elgar.* The Music of the Masters Series. Edited by Wakeling Dry. Published by John Lane, London and New York. Price 2s. 6d.

This book is a singular mixture of candid admiration and not always just criticisms. The author afterwards acquired a reputation of " poking fun " at native writers, and it is this element that often prevails in his book on Elgar. The chapters on the *cantatas* and also the one on the *oratorios* are well worth reading. Some of the remarks are severe, but the poor *librettos* of certain of the *cantatas* are exposed. At the end the author attacks Elgar because the composer spoke against " programism." The criticism is clever, but untimely and incidentally exposes the weakness of rigid programme music. As a whole we do not consider the book as worthy of one who afterwards became a great champion of Elgar and received the dedication of the *Pianoforte Quintet* (Op. 84). There is too much of the sarcastic element which Mr. Newman uses against British composers, the same sarcasm that annoys him very much if we level it against Beethoven's magnificent (?) songs.

JAEGER, A. J. *Analytical and Descriptive Notes on the Oratorios—The Dream of Gerontius, The Apostles,* and *The Kingdom.* Published by Novello and Co., London. Price 1s. each book.

These were written by the composer's dear friend and are absolutely indispensable guides to the three greatest *oratorios.* The names of the various motives were of course supplied by the composer, the three books being official and we know of no substitute for them.

GORTON, REV. CANON. *An Interpretation of the Librettos of the Oratorios—The Dream of Gerontius, The Apostles* and *The Kingdom.* Novello and Co. Price 1s. each book.

The author of these was a friend of the composer and the accounts are written with much insight. The three are intensely interesting and are well worthy of study.

THOMPSON, HERBERT. *Analytical Notes on the Cantata Caractacus.* Novello and Co., London. Price 1s.

BENNETT, JOSEPH. *Analytical Notes on the Cantata King Olaf.* Novello and Co., London.

MASON, DANIEL GREGORY. *Contemporary Composers.* Macmillan and Co., London.

This book contains a fine account and " judgment " of Elgar's two *Symphonies.* There is also a hasty and unjust criticism of the *Pomp and Circumstance Military Marches.*

There are one or two other books which contain references or short studies of Elgar, which doubtless the reader will come across when he is seeking books dealing with modern composers generally.

THE PUBLISHERS OF ELGAR'S WORKS.

NOVELLO and Co., London. Symphonies, Concertos, Chamber Music, Orchestral Suites, Oratorios, Cantatas and other large Choral Works, Lighter Pieces (not all), Part-Songs, other Songs. Symphonic Works, *Froissart*, overture ; *In the South*, overture ; *Falstaff*, symphonic study, etc.

BOOSEY and Co., London. *Cockaigne*, overture ; *Pomp and Circumstance*, military marches ; *Coronation Ode*, (containing *Land of Hope and Glory*, also published separately). A number of Songs without Opus number.

SCHOTT and Co., London. A few Early Works, including *Opus* 1 and *Salut D'Amour*. Also *Dream Children* (Op. 46). Songs, *Pansies* and *Woo Thou Sweet Music* (arranged from *Salut D'Amour*. Full List given under this piece, Op. 12).

JOSEPH WILLIAMS and Co., London. Choral Suite, *From the Bavarian Highlands*, *Three Bavarian Dances* for Orchestra. Minuet (Op. 21), for Orchestra.

ASCHERBERG, HOPWOOD and CREW, LTD., London. A few Early Works.

ELKIN and Co., London. *Polonia*, symphonic prelude ; *Carillon*, *The Belgian Flag*, *A Voice in the Desert*, recitations with orchestra ; *The Starlight Express*, fantasy, arranged as a pianoforte suite ; *Carissima*, *Rosemary*, songs from *The Starlight Express* *Echo's Dance*, pianoforte solo, arranged from the *Fan Ballet*.

ENOCH and SONS, London. *The Crown of India*, *The Fringes of the Fleet*, *Inside the Bar*, song.

BREITKOPF and HARTEL, late of London. String serenade (Op. 20), *Sospiri*.

EDWIN ASHDOWN, London. One or two Odd Pieces obtainable at this house.

CHAPPELL and Co., LTD., London. *Serenade Lyrique*.

INDEX

This index is intended to serve as a reference to any of Elgar's works when occasion arises. Any particular one may be easily found in this book, for the compositions are treated in order of opus number. The appended list will be recognised as a convenient index when only the title of a work can be recalled by the reader.

NAME.	OPUS NO.	NAME.	OPUS NO.
2. The Little Bells (Scherzino).		Was it Some Golden Star?	59
3. Moths & Butterflies (Dance).		When the Spring Comes Round (From A Voice in the Desert)	77
4. Fountain Dance.			
5. The Tame Bear.			
6. The Wild Bears.			

Works without Opus number, i.e., with title only, will be found at the end of the book, commencing after the last work with Opus number has been discussed.